MONTAGU, Jeremy. The world of medieval & Renaissance musical instruments. Overlook (dist. by Viking), 1976. 136p ill bibl index 76-5987. 20.00 ISBN 0-87951-045-5
MUNROW, David. Instruments of the Middle Ages and Renaissance. Oxford, 1976. 95p ill. 12.95 ISBN 0-19-321321-4

These two volumes encompassing the same fairly specialized material, limiting themselves to the same historical period, and arranging their contents within similar categories work well together. With the rapid growth of interest both in performing and in listening to early music (evidenced most dramatically by the burgeoning list of recordings in the Schwann catalogue), libraries are encouraged to add both of these books to their collections. Both authors rely heavily on illustrative material: photographs of historical instruments, illustrations of instruments taken from early manuscripts and treatises, reproductions of medieval and Renaissance art works detailing instruments. All of this pictorial information is immeasurably helpful to the reader. Montagu offers more of a historical chronology of instruments as he works his way from the 6th century to the beginnings of the orchestra in the 16th. How were the instruments played? Who played them? For what occasion? These are some of the questions Monta~~...~~ s and answers; and

Continued

MONTAGU
MUNROW

from the answers he provides, the reader comes away with a wholesome respect for the importance of instrumental music in the life of medieval and Renaissance man. Munrow was not only a virtuoso performer himself on early wind instruments, but he organized the Early Music Consort of London whose recordings are filled with the same kind of verve and authenticity that characterize his writing. His contribution is a *tour de force* of erudition, readability, and excitement; and he brings it about through a prose style that patronizes neither the scholar nor the amateur. That a historical monograph can serve so well such a disparate audience is due in part to Munrow's personal involvement with the instruments he writes about and the insights he provides. These, coupled with historical perspective, give to the reader an understanding and appreciation of the problems involved in playing pre-Baroque instruments. Alas this very talented young man died last May.

Jeremy Montagu has played early music for
many years and was the first to make recon-
structions of early percussion instruments,
on which he has written two books.
He is well known as a lecturer in colleges,
schools and music clubs in Britain and USA
and has made numerous appearances on
television with instruments from his
extensive collection.
He is the author of many articles in
periodicals and encyclopaedias on
instruments from the whole world.

The World of Medieval & Renaissance Musical Instruments

Eric Halfpenny and the late R. Morley Pegge first revealed to me that music sounds right only when it is played on the instruments for which it was originally conceived. To them, with affection, gratitude and respect, this book is dedicated.

The World of Medieval & Renaissance Musical Instruments

Jeremy Montagu

David & Charles
Newton Abbot London Vancouver

ISBN 0 7153 7280 7

© Jeremy P. S. Montagu 1976

All rights reserved. No part of this
publication may be reproduced, stored
in a retrieval system, or transmitted,
in any form or by any means, electronic,
mechanical, photocopying, recording or
otherwise, without the prior permission
of David & Charles (Publishers) Limited

Set in 11 on 12 Bembo
and printed in Great Britain
by Biddles Limited, Guildford, Surrey
for David & Charles (Publishers) Limited
Brunel House   Newton Abbot   Devon

Published in Canada
by Douglas David & Charles Limited
1875 Welch Street North Vancouver BC

Contents

List of illustrations

All photographs not otherwise acknowledged are those of the institutions or places named

Introduction

The earliest medieval music that we hear in the concert hall, on records and over the radio comes from the twelfth century. This is because we know very little about the types of music performed on ordinary occasions and for secular purposes before that date. Church music from the earlier periods has come down to us, but in a notation so imprecise that there is continual controversy over the reconstruction of its sound. Musical notation, although far clearer today than in the early Middle Ages, remains imprecise. Scholars argue about how Mozart performed his own music and no two performances of twentieth-century music are exactly alike. If we cannot agree on the interpretation of music two decades or two centuries old, it is, perhaps, not surprising that we do not know how to perform music a thousand years old. But, however ignorant we may be of the precise meaning of the notation used, we can form some ideas of the sonority of the music, of its actual sound. There are some descriptions of the instruments used; there are some pictures and carvings showing instruments being played in different combinations; there are some surviving instruments, and it is with these that music was made.

Written descriptions are usually imprecise. The names given for the instruments are vague, often inexact and sometimes contradictory. Because more work has been done on Roman and pre-Roman archaeology than on the medieval period, we have more Roman and earlier instruments than we have medieval or early renaissance and those that we do have are often broken and with parts missing. The pictures and the carvings are therefore often the best and the most accurate sources of information, though there also we must tread warily. Many of the illustrations come from bibles and psalters in which instruments may be grouped together, not because they were used together in medieval times but because they were associated with one of the Latin names which St Jerome assigned to the Hebrew terms in, for example, Psalm 150, or to the Chaldaic terms describing Nebuchadnezzar's orchestra in the Book of Daniel. Considerations of symbolism and of numerology also affect the reliability of the pictures, while the imagination of the artist, or his lack of skill in drawing, may distort the appearance of the instruments themselves, as in the Isenheim Altarpiece by Mathias Grünewald.

Often we do not know the names assigned to instruments in any one time or place. Henry Holland Carter's *Dictionary of Middle English Musical Terms* is an invaluable source but, inevitably, it depends upon the information given in the sources quoted, which are often vague and occasionally illusory. The early fourteenth-century Dutch treatise on astrology, Sloane 3983 in the British Library (plates II & III), is exceptional in that it gives the current Latin names for all the instruments which it illustrates. Often a name is comparatively meaningless: Calamis, for example, can be an instrument played with a reed, like our oboe or clarinet, it can mean an instrument made of a reed, such as a flute, or it can mean both, such as the Welsh pibcorn. We shall use contemporary names where possible, but will also use accepted group names, such as shawm, fiddle or rotta, even though they may not have been used in the period we are describing. We shall give common equivalents in other languages but only where they are sufficiently different from the English or other basic name that they might cause confusion. We shall not, for example, trouble to give violino as the Italian equivalent of violin, nor Krummhorn as the German for crumhorn.

   With so much for introduction, let us see how much we can discover of the instruments available to the musicians of the sixth to the eleventh centuries, the period when Europe was emerging from the Dark Ages but was still living on the cultural capital inherited from the Roman Empire, even though it was distorted and dissipated by successive waves of invading marauders from the north and from the east.

Chapter 1
The Early Middle Ages

How our instruments began—
the remains of Greece and Rome

Plate 1 *Above:* Psalm 149: lyre, hand drum and harp. *Below:* Psalm 150: lyre, kithara, hand drum, harp; lyre, tong cymbals, trumpets; hydraulic organ. (The Utrecht Psalter [*f 83*] *University Library Utrecht 32*) Rheims, *c.* 825

Plate 2 (*Right*) King David with rotta and his musicians with two hand-stopped horns, two longer horns and two dancers clapping. (*British Library, Cotton Vespasian A.i* [*f 30v.*]) Probably Canterbury, 8th century

String Instruments

The Kithara

As Emanuel Winternitz has demonstrated, by late Roman times the ancient Greek kithara, the large, professional musician's lyre, had radically changed its shape from that of a lyre to that of a long-necked lute. The tesselated pavement, which he illustrates, from Qasr el-Lebia, dating from the sixth century AD and the *Utrecht Psalter* (plate 1, second from the left in the upper left-hand group below the text), which was written c. 825 near Rheims but which, in its illustrations, reveals earlier Byzantine influence, show the Dark Age form of the kithara. The derivation from the classical lyre is apparent in plate 1 from the shape of the body and from the small wings which project from the top of the body at the root of the neck. These wings we shall recognise again when we look at the fourteenth-century gittern and the sixteenth-century cittern, both of which instruments, along with our modern guitar, owe their existence, as well as their names, to Apollo's kithara.

The Rotta

The Greeks did not invent the lyre; they either acquired it as they passed through Central Asia in their migrations, or else they imported it from the Near East after their arrival in Greece. Whether the Germanic peoples also acquired it as they migrated into Europe, or whether they adopted it from the Greeks or the Romans, we do not, at present, know. It is possible that the lyre was carried into northern Europe from Constantinople during the late Roman Empire, for many of the Byzantine armies, especially the Imperial Bodyguard, were recruited from the Germans or from other northern peoples. We can be certain that the lyre was used in Germany in the sixth century, even though the best evidence for this, the famous Allemanic lyre—once in the Berlin Museum für Völkerkunde and the only complete instrument ever found—was destroyed during the last war. The lyre was also played in Anglo-Saxon Britain, for among the magnificent jewellery and other objects in the royal ship burial of c. 670 at Sutton Hoo, were found a few fragments of something that appeared to be a musical instrument. This was restored at first as a wholly improbable harp, of a shape unknown in any place or time, but it has been more recently, and much more convincingly, reconstructed as a lyre (plate 3) on the model of the Allemanic instrument. This traditional form of the lyre can be seen also in the *Utrecht Psalter* (plate 1, top centre) and in plate 2, from a psalter of the eighth century.

A lighter lyre is shown both to the left and to the right of the lower groups in plate 1. This page of the *Utrecht Psalter* illustrates two psalms: the upper picture is for Psalm 149, the text of which follows it; the lower picture illustrates Psalm 150, the text being on the following page. Psalm 149, v 3 refers to chorus, tympanum and psalterium, translated in the Authorised Version as the dance, the timbrel and the harp. The Sutton Hoo type of lyre was variously known as choros (hence its use to illustrate the word which the Authorised Version more accurately translates as dance), chrotta, rotta, cruit, croud and in Wales into modern times as the crwth, the 'w' being pronounced as 'oo' in Welsh. In the earlier Middle Ages the rotta was plucked, either with a plectrum or with the fingers. By the tenth century,

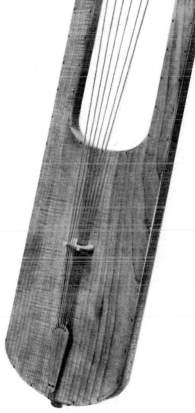

Plate 3   Reconstruction of the lyre from the Sutton Hoo ship burial, 7th century. (*British Museum*)

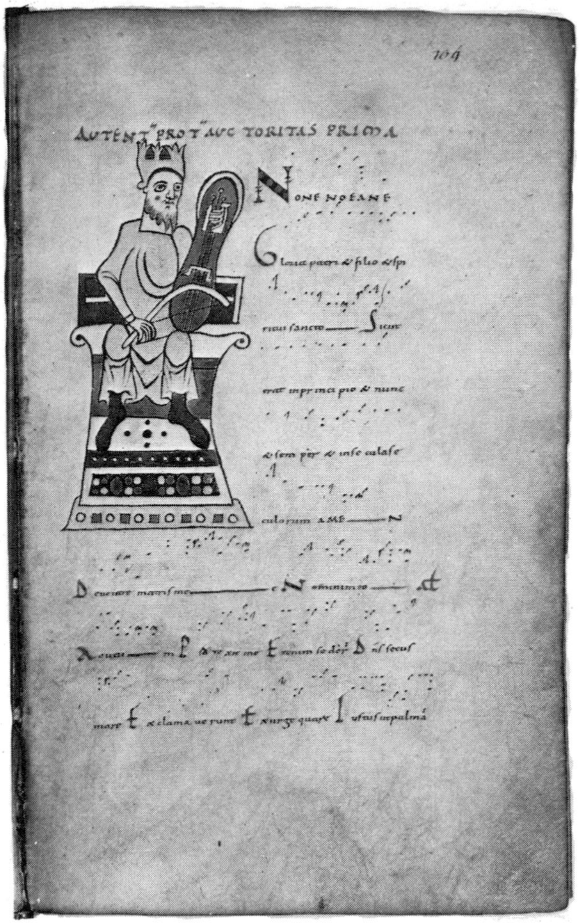

Plate 4 King David with three-stringed bowed rotta. (*Bibliothèque Nationale, Paris, latin 1118 [ƒ 104]*) Southern France, *c.* 1000

and it is impossible to be sure of the number of strings. The early harp was tuned diatonically, with only seven strings to each octave, and could play in only one key unless the player stopped for long enough to tune his F strings to F sharp and so on. Since the harp was used mainly as a bardic instrument, to accompany the player's chanting of the lays, history and sagas of his people, this was no hardship; the bard would tune the instrument to the key which suited his voice and the mode of the lay on which he was about to embark. In this connexion, it must never be forgotten that such lays as *Beowulf*, like the earlier Homeric poems and the later Arthurian romances, were always sung and never read; the music enlivened and illustrated the text and served both as a mnemonic, to remind the bard of what came next, and as a cover, a 'till-ready' in modern terms, while he improvised or sorted out in his mind the next passage. In the early days, this rôle fell to the lyre and the rotta, but by the period with which we are dealing, the harp was becoming the bardic instrument *par excellence*. It is said that it was the Irish who became the bards of Europe, travelling from court to court and from monastery to monastery, earning their living, as the Homeric poets had done before them, by the excellence of their singing and playing. It is claimed that the Irish reinvented the triangular harp, which had been known to the ancient Greeks but which had fallen into disuse, but the evidence seems to be that the type of harp shown in plate 1 was common in other parts of Europe before it was known in Ireland.

The Monochord

One of the few instruments that has been used continuously from the classical Greek period, through the Middle Ages and the Renaissance and down to the present day, is the monochord. This is a theoretician's tool, devised according to legend by Pythagoras himself, who used it to determine the ratios of the pitches of the scale, and it has continued to be used for acoustical research and experiment ever since. The church fathers also employed it to teach choristers to sing and, in this function, it was the ancestor of two separate instruments, the organistrum and the clavichord. The monochord consists of a wooden, rectangular box, usually with one string running along the top surface. A fixed bridge

as Werner Bachmann has shown, the bow was spreading across Europe and the bowed rotta was coming into common use. When the rotta was bowed, there was usually a central fingerboard as in plate 4. It was this type of instrument that led directly to the crwth in Wales and to what Otto Andersson has called the bowed harp in Scandinavia.

The Harp

It is in this early period that King David is usually shown playing an instrument akin to the lyre that would have been used in ancient Israel. In the later Middle Ages and in the Renaissance, he normally plays or tunes a triangular harp with a resonating box, a neck and a forepillar, an instrument which did not exist in his own time, but which came into use in the ninth century (plate 1, both groups). All the early illustrations of the harp are rudimentary at each end defines the sounding length of the string and the player either stops the string at selected points with a rod or tangent while plucking the string with a quill, or else he moves a third bridge along the surface of the box to alter the sounding length of the string; the upper surface of the box was usually marked with the positions for each note.

The Organistrum

The organistrum, which was first described by Odo of Cluny in the tenth century, differed from the normal monochord in two particulars: the string was rubbed by a wheel, so producing a continuous sound, and a second player operated the keys which stopped the string. The key was a bar passing through the neck of the instrument from side to side, with a knob projecting towards the player by which he could turn it, and with a flattened, wider area under the strings. When the key was turned, this wider part revolved upwards and came into contact with the strings, so stopping their vibrating length at that point. In this way, the player could control the length of the string and hence its pitch. This mechanism was clumsy and slow-moving but it was adequate for teaching and for accompanying the church chants of the period. The organistrum was often made with more than one string so that the music sounded in parallel octaves or fifths, just as it did on the contemporary organ, and there is reason to believe that the organ and the organistrum were regarded as interchangeable, so much so that in a number of literary references we are not sure which instrument is being referred to. These references indicate that the organistrum was used from the ninth century at least until the late twelfth century, when the *York Psalter* was drawn and in which it can be seen in the bottom right hand corner of plate 8.

Other Strings

By the ninth century, various instruments of the lute/guitar family were known. Sometimes they appear to have been carved from one baulk of timber, such as the instrument with six strings in plate 5; sometimes they appear to have been made as a box on the end of a neck, like that in plate I, a type of instrument encountered mainly in the Iberian peninsula. North of the Pyrenees, a more common shape was that of the rebec or lira which

can be seen in plate 6. The rebec also was carved from a single block of wood but it had a more smoothly curved outline than the instrument in plate 5, much like half a pear. All three of these instruments were, to begin with, played by plucking the strings with a plectrum (plate 5) or with the fingers. From the tenth century onwards, all three were also bowed, as can be seen in plates 6 and I.

Plate 5   Psalm 150: horn, six-stringed 'lute', tong cymbals, organ with three men blowing. (The Stuttgart Psalter [*f 163v.*] *Stuttgart Landes-B. Bibliothek, fol. 23*) St Germain-des-Prés, *c. 830*

Percussion Instruments

In the psalters—which, as we have already said, are so often the best sources for information—there is usually an introductory picture, often illustrating King David and his musicians, as in plates 2 and 6. There are frequently also illustrations showing musicians accompanying, particularly, Psalms 81 (tympanum, psalterium, cithara, tuba; Authorised Version: timbrel, harp, psaltery, trumpet), 149 (listed above) and 150 (tuba, psalterium, cithara, tympanum, chorus, chordae, organum, cymbala; Authorised Version: trumpet, psaltery, harp, timbrel, stringed instruments, organs, cymbals).

The cymbals were usually small instruments fixed to the ends of tong clappers and were played with one pair in each hand. It has been suggested that the round objects waved in the air in the lower right-hand corner of plate 1 are such tong cymbals; the *Stuttgart Psalter*, dating from *c.* 830 and probably written in Paris (plate 5), provides a better illustration. Other percussion instruments used in this period were drums ('tympanum'), almost the only illustrations of which are the hourglass-shaped instruments played with the hands on plate 1, and bells. Bells were either made by folding a sheet of iron or bronze into a round or square beehive shape and fixing it with rivets, or by casting a similar shape or a bowl of bronze. They were used both as animal bells, as cow bells still are, and for religious purposes as well as in sets (plate 8) for playing music.

Wind Instruments

Horns and Trumpets

Horns and trumpets appear in two iconographic contexts: some are used as melodic instruments, as suggested by the psalms which refer to them, and others are used to signal the Day of Judgement. The latter instruments, which were known as bemen, are often long and curved, as in the lower part of plate 1, the right-hand side of plate 2 and in plate 5. The melodic instruments are shorter, sometimes with finger holes and sometimes with the bells, the wider end, partly stopped by the hand, as can be seen on the left-hand side of plate 2. This hand-stopping, as on the eighteenth-century French horn, lowers the pitch so that different notes can be obtained. A horn with finger holes can be seen on plate 6, from a French psalter of *c.* 1060. This illustration of King David and his musicians shows an interesting mixture of instruments. King David plays a lyre of almost classical Greek type; the long rod on the right is a tuning key. The upper left-hand figure blows a horn with finger holes; the three lines protruding from the bell represent air or sound coming out, a common pictorial device with horns. Below him is a harp of a pattern which was common

a century or so later, with a lion head finial; the object in the harper's left hand is, again, a tuning key. The harp is misdrawn in that the strings should go from the neck to the sound board (the element nearest to the player's body) and not, as they do, to the forepillar; the result of the misdrawing is that the shortest string is the furthest from the player whereas it should be the nearest. The player on the upper right has a set of panpipes of a type common a century or two earlier. The one on the lower right has a three-string rebec or lira which is, with the horn, the only one of the instruments shown that one would expect at this period. The finger-hole horn, which was the ancestor of the cornett, one of the main solo instruments of the Renaissance, is still used as a folk instrument in Sweden, where it is played for dance music with a technique which combines the use of finger holes and hand-stopping the bell. No medieval finger-hole horns are known to survive, but the pictures suggest that they were made from cow or goat horns, as the Swedish instruments are today.

The longer horns and trumpets were probably made either from wood or from metal; many are so large (plates 1 and 5) that they cannot have been made from animal horns. They are normally shown (as in plate 2, right-hand side) with bands round them which may be either decorative, or functional in that they may be holding joints together. The only long trumpet known to have survived is that which was found with the Oseberg Viking ship of the ninth century. This instrument is nearly four feet long and almost cylindrical; it was made by splitting the wood lengthways, hollowing it out and re-uniting it, the two halves being held together with bands similar to those shown on the trumpets in plate 2. Instruments as widely conical as that in plate 5, and the bemen shown in many other illustrations of this period, must have been made of metal. They would presumably have been signal instruments, capable only of a few notes and not intended for musical performances.

Shorter horns were also used as signal instruments, for the hunting field and for warfare. The Bayeux Tapestry shows both functions in a number of its panels and many medieval legends, including those of Charlemagne and Roland at Roncevaux, attest to these uses. Ceremonial instruments of this type,

Plate 6   King David with lyre
and his musicians with harp,
finger-hole horn, panpipe and
rebec. (*Bibliothèque Nationale,
Paris, latin 11550* [*f 7v.*])
St Germain-des-Prés, *c.* 1070

made of elephant tusks and therefore called oliphants, survive in some quantity, at least three of them being said to be the instrument used by Roland. Many were simply princely gifts or possessions, but sometimes they symbolised a more valuable gift, replacing the conventional charter. One of the finest examples of the charter horn is the Horn of Ulph (plate 7) in the Treasury of York Minster. This oliphant was given by King Canute to Ulph Thoroldsson as a symbol of possession of lands and estates, and Ulph, in turn, gave the oliphant to the cathedral along with the same lands. Many other charter horns survive, some medieval and some renaissance. In some cases it was sufficient merely to possess the horn; in others, the holder was obliged to appear before his liege at certain times and blow the horn; normally three times, a magic number through the ages.

Woodwind

As we have mentioned above (plate 6), panpipes were used in this period. These are a row of flutes stopped at the lower end, each one shorter than the next so that each produces a different pitch. A melody can be played by moving the mouth along the line in much the same way that we do with the mouthorgan. In the Middle Ages, the panpipes were usually either a series of cane tubes held in a wooden case or a series of bores drilled side by side into one piece of wood. Open-ended flutes with finger holes were also known, usually quite short with three, four or five finger holes in the side of the tube, and blown from the end via a duct, in the same way as the recorder or the penny whistle. Various fragments have been found, from prehistoric times onwards,

Plate 7   The Horn of Ulph, 11th century oliphant. (*York Minster*)

but very few complete instruments and even fewer that can be securely dated. The majority of those known to us are made of bone, often a sheep's or deer's leg bone, but this is not necessarily because bone was the commonest medieval material. It is probable that cane or wood, especially those woods such as elder which have a natural tube, were the more common as well as the earlier, but bone survives long burial in the earth, whereas wood and reed quickly rot away to nothing.

Of the other woodwind instruments we know much less. On the rare occasions that they are illustrated, the shapes are so indeterminate that it is impossible to be sure what they are. The Paris troper from which plate 4 is taken shows a number of wind instruments, all of which are illustrated in Tilman

Seebass's study of this manuscript, but none of which are identifiable with any degree of certainty. It is probable that they are varieties of reed instruments such as the chalumeaux, instruments of cylindrical bore with single reeds similar to those now used on the drone pipes of Scottish bagpipes.

The Organ

One wind instrument which was used from Roman times onwards was the organ. This had been invented in the third century BC in Alexandria and was known throughout the Roman Empire both as a large instrument for use in the circus and as a small instrument for houses of entertainment. The only surviving Roman instrument, in the city of Aquincum on the outskirts of modern Budapest, was found in what seems to have been a brothel. The organ gradually came into use in the Christian church and was already popular and not uncommon by Carolingian times, as Perrot points out. Plate 1 shows that the ancient hydraulic organ, the air pressure of which was stabilised by water pressure, was still known in the ninth century. The detailed descriptions of the great organ at Winchester in the tenth century, as well as various instruction books and illustrations such as plate 5, in which an organ can be seen on the right-hand side, tell us that pneumatic organs, without the stabilising water cylinders, were also used. Three organ blowers, with their feet on bellows and holding a rail with their hands behind their backs to keep their balance, are visible in plate 5 and it is probable that there were three more on the other side of the organ, out of the picture. A contemporary description says that seventy men performed this function at Winchester. Since the organ at this period had no sliding stops to shut off the air from some of the ranks of pipes, all the pipes associated with one note on the keyboard sounded together. Thus, no contrast was possible and the full organ, with all the octave and mixture ranks, sounded the whole time. Organ music was usually slow-moving, because the keyboard, unlike the modern levers which require only an ounce or two of pressure from the finger, consisted of sliders which had to be pulled out to sound a note and pushed back to silence it.

The Rôle of the Musician

The musician of the early Middle Ages seems usually to have been the minstrel, either resident in a large establishment or travelling from one establishment to another, singing the lays and the sagas to his own accompaniment. Most of the illustrations of groups of musicians are associated with ecclesiastical usage, though it would seem likely that when individual minstrels found themselves in the company of others at fairs and like occasions they might have joined together to play for secular purposes also. In addition to the minstrels, there were the jongleurs, the animal trainers, the acrobats and the other entertainers, all of whom included music among their other activities: acrobats performed to music, as did jugglers; bears danced to music and people also required dance music. What records and

Plate 8 King David tuning a harp and his musicians with double bell chime, rebec, waisted fiddle, triple duct flute, indeterminate instrument, psaltery, hand bells, organistrum (The York Psalter [f 21v.] *Glasgow University Library, Hunterian 229*) York, c. 1175

illustrations there are of this period are scanty, but it is clear that the professional musicians were already regarded as low class, as rogues and vagabonds, as they were to remain even into modern times. The only period in which, to some extent, this was untrue was that ensuing, in which, exceptionally, there came into being a group of aristocratic professional musicians, known as the troubadours in Provence and the trouvères in the rest of France. These musicians had the same skills as the jongleurs and the minstrels of their day, but many of them were of the same rank as those whom they entertained. Neither before nor since has it been possible for the aristocratic musician to avoid being either *déclassé* or regarded as an incompetent amateur aping the professional, irrespective of his skill and his proficiency.

Chapter 2
The Crusades

The Age of Chivalry to the Black Death

Twelfth century to 1350

From the middle of the eleventh century, a new atmosphere developed in Europe; this was a time of intellectual awakening and of a desire for new knowledge. Although political rivalries between prince and prince and between the secular powers and the church continued, a sense of Europe as an entity began to emerge. One of the first results was a campaign of colonial conquest. The Crusades may have been initiated from spiritual motives but an almost immediate result was the establishment of European colonies in the Middle East. As in all colonial enterprises, trade followed the flag and merchants, particularly the Venetians, were able to set up their own trading bases in the Levant under the protection of the Crusaders.

From the eighth century, Spain had been occupied by the Muslims; now other Muslim lands were occupied by Europeans. There were thus two points of contact with the Islamic world, a world which had retained many of the arts and sciences of Greek and Roman civilisation which had been lost in the European Dark Ages. Because of the desire for new knowledge, these contacts bore rapid fruit. The Graeco-Arabic traditions of philosophy crossed the Pyrenees from the schools of Spain to those of Paris and inspired the foundation of the major universities of Europe and the partial liberation of learning from the rigid control of the Church. From the same source came the medieval sciences, the names of some of which are Arabic to this day, such as alchemy and algebra, and others, such as arithmetic and astrology, which retained their ancient Greek styles.

With learning and with the sciences came the arts of literature and music. The historical saga of the minstrel gave way to the romance of the troubadour, into which was woven the concept of knightly chivalry, the theory that the brutal and licentious soldiery were in fact the protectors of the innocent and the servants of God and of their selected ladies, who acquired some of their aura of sanctity as a reflection of the cult of the Virgin Mary. The aim of the troubadours in their romances, such as the Arthurian legends, was to inculcate these chivalric virtues and to a great extent they succeeded; it might be said that chivalry was disseminated by the troub-

adours and they persuaded their hearers to behave like their heroes.

The romances, like the earlier sagas, were chanted and sung, not read as we read them today. They were accompanied by instruments and many of these instruments were new. New instruments came across the Pyrenees; others were brought back from the Middle East as the armies and the traders travelled to and fro. Some instruments reveal by their names that they came from the Islamic world: the lute, the rebec, the canon, the añafil, the shawm, the nakers. These and others can be seen still in use in that world today and can be seen in European art from the twelfth century onwards.

As in the earlier period, only a bare handful of instruments survive and most of our knowledge is derived from the illustrations in manuscripts and from the carvings in churches. One of the most important sources is a pair of manuscripts dating from *c.* 1270, a set of poems gathered together or written by King Alfonso X of Spain, called The Wise, the *Cantigas de Santa Maria*. One of the manuscripts, Escorial T.j.1, contains only a few illustrations of musical instruments, one of the most informative of which is our plate 9. The other, Escorial J.b.2, the better known of the two, has forty miniatures, one for every ten cantigas, and all of them show instruments; twenty of these will be found here. The others show instruments which were used, and some indeed are still used, as folk instru-

Plate 9   Oval fiddle, three psalteries of different shapes, shawm. (Cantigas de Santa Maria [*Cantiga 120*] *Escorial T.j.1*) Seville, *c.* 1280

ments but which did not enter the main stream of European music. Most of the instruments in the *Cantigas* derive from the Muslim world and many of them are clearly ancestral to instruments which were used throughout Europe in the succeeding centuries. We in Europe are incurable meddlers and are always trying to change things to see whether we can make them work better or differently, so that our instruments, along with all our other artifacts, are ever changing. In other parts of the world, people prefer to leave things as they are and to perfect their use, rather than to change their form. Thus, although many of these instruments have changed very considerably in Europe, we can still find many instruments identical with those illustrated in the *Cantigas* in other areas which have also drawn their culture from the Muslim world. Comparison between these surviving instruments and the illustrations confirms the general reliability of this source and the accuracy of its miniatures.

String Instruments

A glance at the illustrations to this chapter (plates II–V and 8–41) reveals that the most important instruments from the twelfth to the fourteenth centuries were the strings, a fact which is ignored in most modern performances of medieval music. This was a period of individuality, of experimentation and, as the new string instruments swept across Europe, of gradual change until, eventually, the instruments which were to last through the Renaissance and into the Baroque were established. Although the basic types were known and generally accepted in the thirteenth century, details varied from one instrument to the next, for players either made their own instruments or commissioned craftsmen to make exactly what they wanted. Certain features gradually became standard, as their advantages were recognised by more and more players, until stable types of instruments came into almost universal use throughout Europe.

The Fiddle

The fiddle (English *fithel*, German *fidel*, French *vielle*, Italian *viola*, Spanish *vihuela*, all deriving from a common root, the Latin *fidicula*) began as a spade-shaped or more often oval instrument (plates I, II, III, 9, 10, 11, 12, 17), later becoming rectangular in shape with rounded corners. Sometimes the instrument was waisted to a greater or a lesser extent, sometimes so much so that the shape was that of the figure 8 (plates IV, 8, 13). The strings, of which there were normally from three to five, were tensioned by pegs inserted either from the front or the back, occasionally both (plate III), of a round, oval or leaf-shaped peg-board or peg-box; the laterally inserted pegs such as we use on the violin were found only on the rebecs and the lutes. Tuning pegs were normally T-headed but other shapes, for

23

Plate 12 Oval fiddles, one with
three and one with four strings.
(Cantigas [ƒ 193ν.] Escorial J.b.2)

instance the trefoil heads in plate II, were not
uncommon. There was usually a finger board on
the neck, but this is not always shown and it is by no
means certain that the omission was due to careless-
ness by the artist. The finger board often carried
frets, presumably made as in the Renaissance by
tying lengths of gut round the neck. The strings
terminated at a wooden tail piece, tied to the bottom
end of the body with gut (plate II) and were supported
by a bridge which transmitted their vibrations to the
wood of the belly. It seems likely that the bridge and
the tail piece were sometimes combined, as in plate II,
though illustrations are seldom sufficiently clear to be
certain whether tail piece and bridge were two pieces
of wood side by side or whether they were one
L-shaped piece of wood. Early and Moorish fiddles
had bellies of skin, as can be seen in the plates from
the *Cantigas*, but this was later replaced in northern
European fiddles by a plate of wood; the use of skin
for the belly seems never to have been popular north
of the Pyrenees, probably because skin does not hold
its tension in a damp northern climate and a soft
belly gives a dull sound. The belly had a sound hole
cut in it, often a central, round hole, with or without
inserted tracery such as we find on the later lute, and
with or without smaller sound holes near the corners.
As time went on, a pair of D-shaped holes became
the more usual form of sound holes, one on each side
of the line of the strings. The bridge can stand
between a pair of D holes, whereas the central round
hole has the disadvantage that the bridge must either
be close against the tail piece or near to the finger
board. When the bridge is close to the finger board,
the sounding length of the strings, from the peg-
board nut to the bridge, is excessively short for the
size of the instrument and the sound hole is in an
acoustically ineffective position; as a result such
instruments were rarely used. The lower position
was the more practical of the two and can often be
seen in pictures, although this, too, can be inefficient
acoustically.

The bows that were used varied from the long and
slender to the short and thick and from the almost
straight to the nearly semi-circular. It is probable
that the short bows were of wood sufficiently rigid
that their arc was fixed; the tension of the bow hair
would then need to be controlled by some form of
tensioning device or by the player's fingers. The

Plate I   Oval fiddle with five strings. (The Silos Apocalypse [*f86*] *British Library, Add 11695*) Mozarabic, Castile, 1109

Plate II   *Upper panel:* 'Musician sounding together the drum and the golden shawm'. The drum is a timbre with snare and five pairs of jingles. Also a four-stringed oval fiddle 'Viola'.

Lower panel: 'An armed man seeking skill and pleasure with various instruments of music'. Three-stringed oval fiddle and bow, five-stringed citole, harp, symphony. (*British Library, Sloane 3983* [*f 15*]) Dutch astrological treatise, early 14th century

Plate III   Venus playing a psaltery with fifteen strings. *Left:* three-stringed oval fiddle and bow; *right:* mandore. (*Sloane 3983* [*f 42v.*])

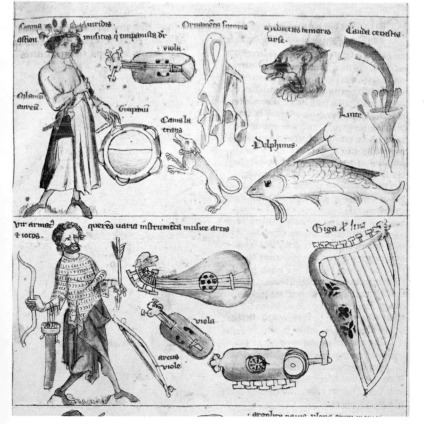

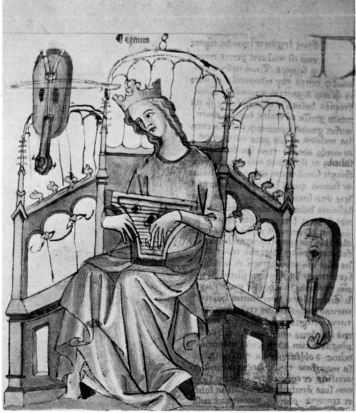

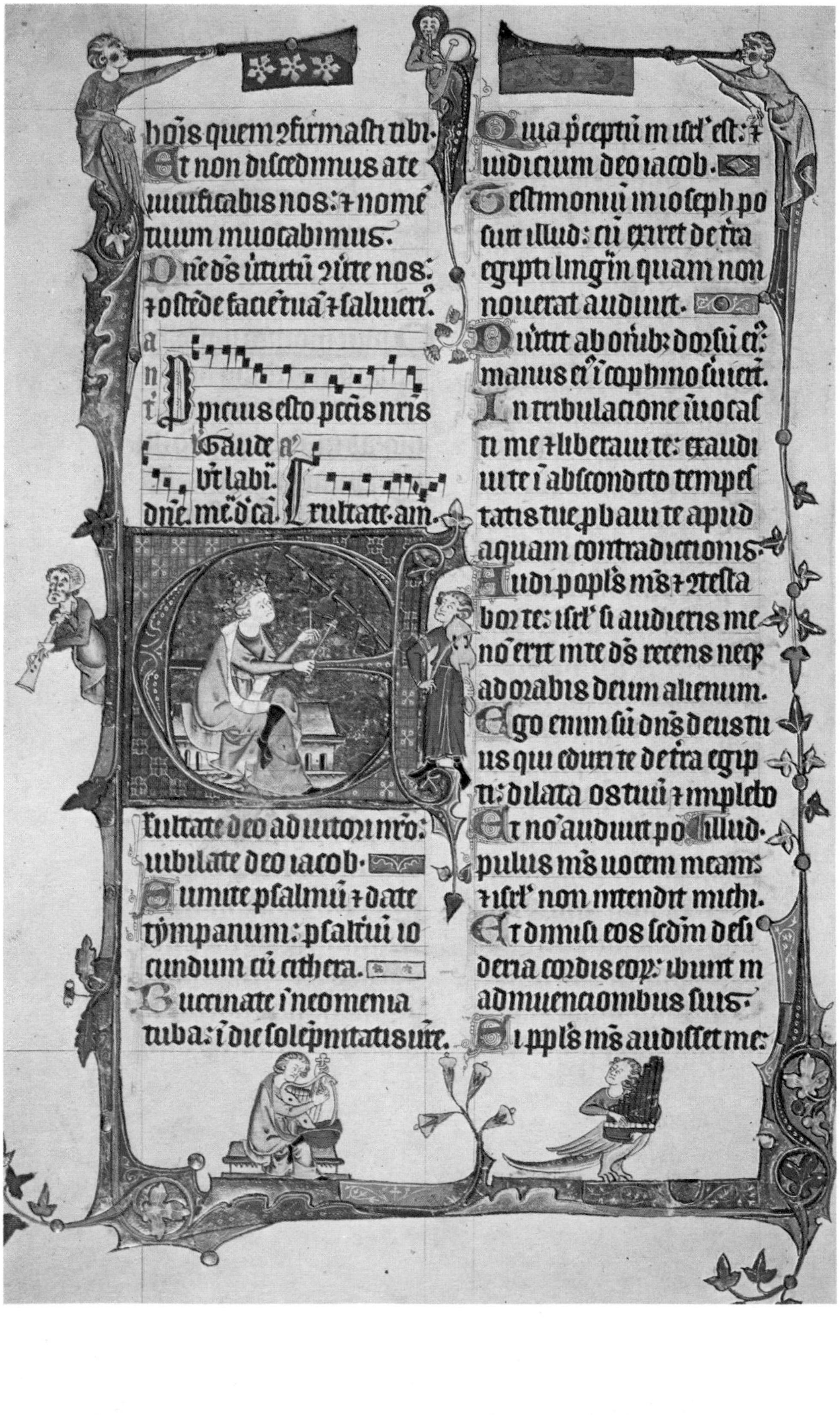

hois quem confirmasti tibi:
Et non discedimus a te
viuificabis nos: et nome
tuum inuocabimus.
Dñe ds virtutu conuerte nos:
et ostede faciem tua et salui eri.

ant. Propicius esto peccatis nris...
Gaude... vt labi...
dñe. me dca. Exultate am.

Exultate deo adiutori nro:
iubilate deo iacob.
Sumite psalmu et date
tympanum: psalteriu io
cundum cu cithera.
Buccinate in neomenia
tuba: in die solempnitatis vre.

Quia preceptu in isrl est: et
iudicium deo iacob.
Testimoniu in ioseph po
suit illud: cu exiret de tra
egypti linguam quam non
nouerat audiuit.
Diuertit ab oneribz dorsu ei:
manus ei in cophino siuerit.
In tribulacione inuocas
ti me et liberaui te: exaudi
ui te in abscondito tempes
tatis tue: pbaui te apud
aquam contradicionis.
Audi popls ms et contesta
bor te: isrl si audieris me
non erit in te ds recens neq
adorabis deum alienum.
Ego enim su dñs deus tu
us qui eduxi te de tra egyp
ti: dilata os tuu et implebo
Et no audiuit populus illud.
pulus ms uocem meam:
et isrl non intendit michi.
Et dimisi eos secundm desi
deria cordis eorum: ibunt in
adinuencionibus suis.
Si populus ms audisset me

Plate 13 Five-stringed waisted fiddle, c. 1270 (*Lincoln Cathedral Angel Choir, N 11*)

longer bows, which usually had a greater length of wood beyond the hair at the nut end, by the player's hand, appear light enough to have been bent into their arcuate form by the tension of the bow hair and so would not require further tensioning in use. There is no evidence at all as to the type of tensioning used on the shorter bows; it is possible that, as on surviving folk instruments, a peg was inserted into the handle to tighten the bow hair just as a peg tightened the strings of the instrument. We can seldom see any details of the bridge. A flat bridge, such as appears to have been normally used until the late fourteenth century, would mean that more than one string was sounded at a time, producing either a drone on a steady pitch or a melody in parallel fourths or fifths, according to whether one or two strings were stopped by the fingers. The latter technique, simple organum in parallel parts, was certainly used by singers, and the former is equally possible, since most music of this period sounds

effective, to our ears at least, with a drone tuned to the pitch of the final note. The popularity of the bagpipe with one or more drones and of other drone instruments confirms that the drone accompaniment was also considered effective in the Middle Ages.

The body of the fiddle seems to have been hollowed out from one piece of wood, as was done on the earlier rebec, with a thin sheet of wood inserted as the belly. Whether the neck and the head were also the same piece of wood, as they were on the rebec, is less certain and less likely. The oval instruments with straight necks, such as can be seen in the *Cantigas*, probably had bodies carved from one piece of wood with a separate rod inserted to act as the neck (plate 12). The larger bodied instruments with comparatively short necks, such as can be seen in plates 13 and 17, are more likely to have been carved from one block. Since no medieval fiddles are known to survive and none of the pictures or carvings are sufficiently detailed to be certain, this remains one of

Plate IV Psalm 81. King David plays five clapper bells with two hammers; others play two long trumpets with banners, pipe & tabor, four-stringed waisted fiddle, droneless bagpipe with conical chanter, harp with high-shouldered sound box, portative organ with nine pipes and keys and frontal bellows. (*British Library, Arundel 83 [f 55v.*])
East Anglian psalter, c. 1310

Plate 14 Three-stringed
mandores or plucked rebecs.
(Cantigas [*f 104.*] *Escorial J.b.2*)

Plate 15 Waisted guitar with
five strings and oval
guitar with five divergent strings.
(Cantigas [*f 147.*] *Escorial J.b.2*)

those many questions which we cannot answer definitely.

When it was first used, the fiddle was played on the knee, as at the right-hand side of plate 8, and this tradition was maintained in the south, as can be seen in the *Cantigas* and in much of the Middle East and the East today. In northern Europe, however, it became customary to hold the fiddle upwards, either across the chest or on the shoulder. The instrument was not gripped under the chin, as we hold the violin, for players used only the first position and did not move the left hand up and down the neck of the fiddle; they could therefore use that hand to support the weight of the instrument as well as to stop the strings on the finger board. Not all players held the instrument in the left hand and the bow in the right; many pictures show players working the other way round and it was only with the rise of the orchestra in the seventeenth century, leading to a desire for uniformity, that the left-handed player became as rare as he is today. The right-handed were, of course, in the majority, as is to be expected in a world in which the majority of people are right-handed.

Rebab and Rebec

The rebab, the Middle Eastern equivalent of the rebec, appears in some of the *Cantigas* miniatures (plate 20) and survives in use today in the Middle East. It had a belly partly or wholly of skin and a body with fairly straight sides and a rounded back which was carved from a solid block. The peg box projected backwards and was made from a separate piece of wood; the pegs were inserted from the sides, like those of the violin. This was an instrument which was little used in northern Europe, unlike the true rebec with its more curved outline, which can be seen on the left-hand side of plate 8, although a corruption of its name, rubible, was the common name for the rebec into the fifteenth century.

Guitar, Citole and Mandore

The instruments in the *Cantigas* which have the closest resemblance to the rebec are those in plate 14, which are plucked and not bowed. These miniatures and other sources reveal that players sounded their instruments in the way that they preferred, some plucking and others bowing. The nineteenth-century theory that the waist of the fiddle and the narrow pear shape of the rebec were introduced for the convenience of the bow has been disproved for, as Bachmann has shown, the waisted plucked instruments are earlier than the introduction of the bow, and the rebec shape goes back at least to 300 BC, for there is a Tanagra statuette in the Louvre of a lady plucking a rebec. The renaissance Spanish terminology indicates that the waisted instruments were all regarded as the same, for all were termed vihuela: *vihuela de mano* for those plucked with the fingers, *vihuela de peñola* for those plucked with a plectrum, usually a quill, and *vihuela de arco* for those which were bowed. These names survive in other languages also, for the guitar is still known as viola in Portugal and the vihuela de arco was known as the viol or viola throughout Europe. The vihuela de peñola, or plectrum guitar, already existed by the time of the miniatures (plates 10 and 15): waisted instruments which are plucked with a plectrum. Their use was confined, initially, to the Iberian peninsula; in the rest of Europe a pear shaped plucked instrument, rather wider across the belly than the rebec, was the more popular. This can also be seen in the *Cantigas*, in plate 15 and perhaps in plate 11, and also in plates II and III from other sources. The citole and the mandore look much alike from the front, the principal difference between them being that the citole had a flat back and the mandore a vaulted back. The citole, in combination with the gittern, was the ancestor of the cittern and of such instruments as the English guitar and Portuguese guitarra of the eighteenth century and later; the mandore led in due course to the various small lutes such as the pandurinas and to the Milanese type of mandoline. It is, however, probably true to say that at this period the two instruments were one which was sometimes made with a flat back and sometimes with a vaulted back, according to the maker's preference; it is also true that from the front, as most instruments are shown in pictures, the two are indistinguishable.

The plucked instruments could have either a raised bridge, like that of the fiddle, or a flat bridge. With a raised bridge, the strings always passed across it and were fixed to a tail piece or to the end of the instrument. When the bridge was flat, sometimes the strings passed across it and were fixed in the same way, as with the mandoline and folk guitar today, but sometimes the bridge was glued to the belly and the strings were tied to it, as with the lute and the modern classical guitar. It was the varying stresses of gut or metal strings which determined which technique was used. Metal strung instruments had their strings fixed to the lower end of the body, simply because their tension would be too great for a glued bridge to be practicable. The pull of the strings would rip it from the belly, whereas the gut strings of the lute and of the guitar were at so much lower a tension that a glued bridge could safely withstand the strain; with gut strings, the player could use whichever type of fixing he preferred. It is tempting to assume that a further difference between citole and mandore was string material, but there is no other evidence than that of their renaissance descendants, by which time the mandores were gut strung and the citterns wire strung, and this assumption can only be hypothetical.

Frets can be seen in some pictures as lines across the finger board (eg plates 10, 15, 17, 20). A question arises when there are no frets in a picture or carving of a similar instrument: was this instrument played without frets, or did the artist not bother to put them in? The likely answer is that some players used frets and some did not, according to the type of sound that they preferred. The purpose of the fret is not to tell the player where to put the fingers but to make a very definite difference to the sound. The finger stopping the string directly on the finger board, without a fret, has a soft edge because of the fleshiness of the finger tip. The finger pressing the string to the finger board immediately behind a fret has a sharp edge because it is the fret, rather than the finger, which forms the cut-off point and terminates the vibrating length of the string. This difference can be observed today on the violin, which has a marked difference in tone quality between the open strings, whose length is terminated by a wooden bar or nut, and the stopped strings, where the fleshy finger terminates the vibrating length of the strings. It was precisely to avoid this difference of tone between stopped and open strings that the viols in the Renaissance were fitted with frets.

The Symphony

We referred before to the use of drones and parallel lines in string instruments. The instrument

Plate 16   Symphonies. (Cantigas
[ƒ 154v.] Escorial J.b.2)

best suited to this style of playing was the symphony,
known in the earlier period as the organistrum and
later to be called hurdy-gurdy. In the eleventh and
twelfth centuries, when the organistrum was still
played by two people, the body shape was often
exactly the same as that of the fiddle (plate 8, bottom
right-hand corner), and not only the shape but all the
features of fiddle and symphony were interchangeable. We find instruments played with a separate
bow whose strings are stopped with tangents like
those of the hurdy-gurdy; the Swedish nyckelharpa
is a surviving example of this and a number of
mediaeval examples are illustrated in Jan Ling's book
on the nyckelharpa; we also find wheel played
instruments with a fiddle-like finger board (eg
Bachmann's plate 85). The great advantage of the
wheel is that the sound may either be continuous or
rhythmically jerky, as the player prefers. In the early
mediaeval period the instrument seems to have been
mainly a church one and in the church services and
in choir training the continuous sound would be
what was required; it is in the later folk usage—once
the churches had become wealthy enough to use
organs instead and had abandoned the instrument to
the folk musicians, as in plates V and 16—that we
may presume that the rhythmic technique, to be

heard today in France and Hungary and elsewhere,
came into use. Sárosi Bálint has published a number
of examples of the use of the rhythmic drone on the
Hungarian instrument.

The device that enabled the symphony to be
played by one person, instead of two, was a key bar
which slid instead of being turned. The bar had fixed
to it a tangent, or wooden blade, which projected
upwards and which touched the string and stopped
it from the side when it was pressed inwards, and a
stud which would prevent it from falling out when
the key was released. Then, provided that the
instrument were held with the keys on the lower side
of the body, the keys could be pushed in to stop the
string and would fall away from it by their own
weight as soon as they were released. This design of
key also had the advantage that as many strings as
were desired could run over the wheel and these
could either sound as drones or be stopped, according to the number of tangents fitted to each key bar.
This type of symphony can be seen in plates II, V
and 16. The artist of the *Luttrell Psalter* (plate V) has
drawn the instrument incorrectly; the keys should
be on the lower side as they are in the other plates.
In plate II some allowance must be made for perspective; the artist has tried to draw the wheel from
a different angle from the rest of the instrument.

The Gittern

The gittern was the northern European equivalent
of the southern guitar. It was almost always built
with wing shaped upper bouts (plates 17 and 19), the
surviving traces of the kithara of the Greek poets, as
was mentioned in the first chapter, though fiddle
shaped upper bouts (plate 18) are sometimes seen.
The head of the instrument was usually turned back
under the finger board as in plate 19 and, allowing
for poor perspective drawing, in plate 17, though
fiddle peg boxes, as in plate 18, were also used, as
were extended heads. The body is thicker at the base
of the neck than at the lower end, a feature which
reappears on the later cittern. There were normally
four strings which were plucked with a heavy
plectrum. Plate 19 shows a copy of one of the very
few surviving fourteenth-century instruments, the
Warwick Castle gittern, which was modernised in
the late sixteenth century into a violin. This copy,
which is in the Victoria and Albert Museum, is

illustrated here in preference to the original because, at the time that it was made at the end of the nineteenth century, the instrument still retained its original gittern bridge, a curved piece of wood covered with the same superb carved ornamentation that enriches the rest of the body; since that date this bridge has been lost and the original instrument, now in the British Museum, is today fitted with a wholly unsuitable modern violin bridge.

The Lute

An instrument which was to be of greater importance than the gittern to future generations was the lute, one of the first appearances of which in a European manuscript can be seen in plate 20. The lute was in use in the Levant by the sixth century AD, when it was known in Sassanid Persia, as can be seen in Farmer's *Islam*. Its name is still Arabic today; *el 'ud* in Arabic became the lute in English. One of the *Cantigas* miniatures (folio 54) shows two lutes much as they were in the sixth century, with sinuous sound holes, slender necks with no visible finger board, no frets and with the strings running in a fan shape; an instrument which is still played in China and Japan. The other *Cantigas* illustration, plate 20, shows a much larger lute with a finger board and frets which, although it still retains some features of the smaller instruments, is much closer to the early European instrument and very close to the modern Middle Eastern 'ud. All three are played with a plectrum, which remained the normal technique for the first few centuries of the lute's life in Europe, as it is still elsewhere. In most of the *Cantigas* miniatures, one player tunes to the other; in plate 20, however, we have a clear illustration of one player accompanying the other.

The lute was one of the most elaborate and most delicate of instruments. The vaulted back was built up from thin staves of wood which were bent into shape and the belly was pierced with one or more sound holes which were filled with carved roses of wooden tracery. The rose is an elaboration of a sound board pierced with small holes and was sometimes carved in the wood of the sound board, though it was later more usually carved from a separate piece of wood and inserted into the belly. It has an important acoustical function, since the area of the open sound hole controls much of the tone quality and it is by no means only a decorative feature. During the later Renaissance and after, other materials were also used for the rose in various instruments, usually either cut paper, bone or metal;

Plate 18 Four-stringed gittern.
(*Lincoln Cathedral Angel Choir,
N 10*)

Plate 19   Electrotype of the
Warwick Castle Gittern,
converted into a violin in the late
16th century. (*Victoria & Albert
Museum, London*)

the lute almost invariably followed the earlier
tradition in having its rose of wood.

The Harp

The harp in the thirteenth and fourteenth centuries
normally remained a light instrument, still diatonically tuned. The sound box had increased somewhat
in size since the earlier period (plates II, IV, 8,
21), swelling out at the shoulder and often with an
ornamental rose filling a sound hole at that point
(plate II). In plate 21, both players have the harp on
the rearmost shoulder; this may be pictorial sym-
metry, or it may be that the harp, like so many other
instruments, was played left- or right-handed as the
player preferred. The harp was one of the most
frequently portrayed instruments of the Middle
Ages, for even the psalters with the minimum of
illumination usually have a King David, often in the
initial B of the first psalm. As with other instruments,
the harps vary in pattern: sometimes we find the
swelling shoulder mentioned above and sometimes
the sound box is straight and narrow, widening
slightly towards the bass end; the fore-pillar is
sometimes straight and sometimes curved or even

Plate 20   Large lute with nine
strings accompanying two-
stringed rebab. (Cantigas [*f 162.*]
Escorial J.b.2)

33

Plate 21   Harps, one played
left-handed. (Cantigas [*f 341.*]
Escorial J.b.2)

Plate 22   King David with Irish
harp with brays. (*Lincoln
Cathedral Angel Choir, S 14*)

sinuous. The strings seldom exceed a dozen or so,
suggesting a range of an octave and a half to two
octaves at the most.

During the second half of the thirteenth century,
a new harp came into use, a far heavier instrument
with a massive sound box, increasing greatly in
width towards the bass, with a strongly arched neck
and a heavily curved fore-pillar. This was to be
known to succeeding generations as the Irish harp
(plate 52) but it is first found in the carvings of the
Angel Choir at Lincoln Cathedral (plate 22), which
date from *c.* 1270 and appear to be earlier than any
Irish illustrations; as yet one cannot say in which
area this type of harp was developed. Plate 22 shows
also the use of brays in the belly of the harp. These
are L-shaped pegs which not only pin the strings
into the belly but whose horizontal arm touches the
string lightly and produces a buzzing sound which
increases the volume considerably and helps the
sound to sustain. These brays seem not to have been
a feature of the harp in Ireland but were used elsewhere in Europe as may be seen in later plates.

The Psaltery

The type of psaltery which is found most frequently in the later Middle Ages (plates III and 23) seems to appear first around the year 1300. Before that date, other shapes were used (plates 8 and 9), one of which (plate 9, right) is clearly the ancestor of the later shape. Some of the other patterns of psaltery survived into the later period in some parts of Europe. The pitch of a string depends upon its length, its mass and its tension and all three of these may be varied. Thus, an instrument may have all its strings the same length and the same mass but all at differing tensions. The disadvantage of such a design is that only two or three strings would be at the optimum tension for tone quality and that the difference of tension from the bass to the treble would almost certainly twist the body of the instrument out of shape. Alternatively, the strings may be of the same length and at similar tension, thus avoiding distortion, but of varying mass and material; this is the solution that has been adopted on the fiddles and lutes and other similar instruments. Another possibility is to keep the mass and tension equal, depending solely on the length of the strings to vary the pitch. This means that the strings must double in length for each octave lower and such instruments (eg the left-hand psaltery in plate 9) are awkward and unwieldy to play. A fourth possibility is to vary both length and mass, while again keeping the tension as even as possible to avoid distortion, and this solution was adopted for the harp, for the later psaltery and eventually for the keyboard instruments. The modern piano, for example, has short, thin strings in the treble and long, heavy strings in the bass. In the thirteenth century, instrument makers were still experimenting, which is why we see these various designs of psaltery. It was quickly realised that the first three designs, as in plate 8 and the left-hand and the central instruments in plate 9, were not practicable and the fourth solution, the combination of differential length and mass, one pattern of which can be seen on the right of plate 9, survived as in plates III and 23. This instrument was sometimes called a canon, from the Arabic *qanun*, or instrumento di porco from its resemblance to a pig's head and snout, and, when divided in half, as the demicanon, micanon or

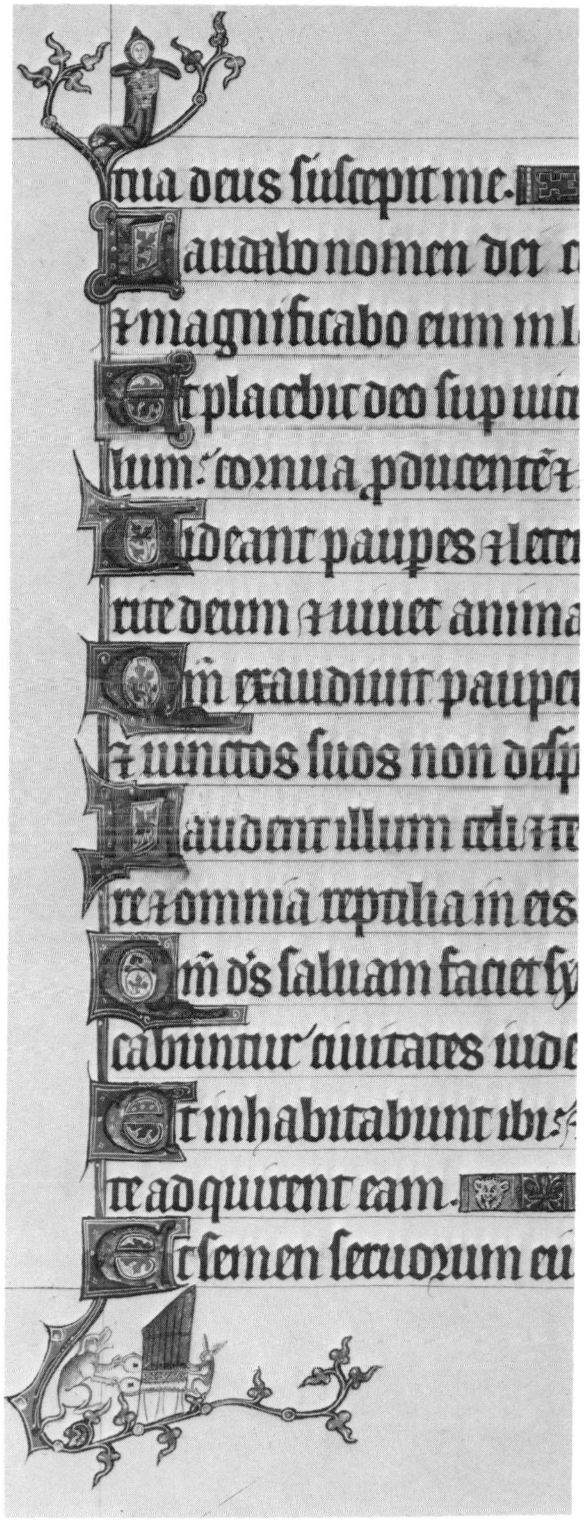

Plate 23 Man playing nine-stringed psaltery and rabbit and dog playing positive organ. (The Gorleston Psalter [f 88v.] British Library, Add 49622) East Anglian, c. 1325

Plate 24   Mass of the Virgin.
Portative organ with castellated
bass pipes and drone pipes at
treble end. (*Dutch book of hours,
British Library, Stowe 17
[ff 22v. & 23]*) Maastricht, *c.* 1300

Plate 25   Portative organ.
(*Cantigas [f 185v.] Escorial J.b.2*)

demiporco. The shape of the micanon or demiporco survives as that of the harpsichord and grand piano. The psaltery was played by plucking, normally with quills though sometimes with the fingers, and the strings ran flat across the instrument from a bridge on each side.

Wind Instruments

The Organ

Two types of small organ were introduced in the thirteenth century, the positive organ and the portative organ. Their tone quality still could not be varied, because the invention of the stop, which allows the organist to shut off some registers and open others, was yet in the future and normally only one rank of pipes was provided. The positive could be carried around by a group of people, but had to be placed in position to be played and needed the assistance of another person on the bellows (plate 23). The portative was so small that it could be carried and played simultaneously by one person. It was usually supported by a strap over the player's shoulder, when standing, or on the knee when sitting, with the left hand operating the bellows and the right hand the keyboard, as in plates IV, V, 24, 25. As the plates show, there was still considerable variety in construction. The types of bellows varied, with some being simply an adapted domestic bellows (plate 25), others being fitted below the instrument (plate IV) and, in the School of Orcagna *Coronation of the Virgin* in the National Gallery in London, which is rather later than those shown, an ingenious double arrangement whereby the left forearm controls a bellows at the back, of the type which was to become standard, and the fingers of the same hand control a smaller bellows beneath the instrument, presumably so as to avoid the pauses between phrases during which the bellows were drawn open to refill them. These breath pauses were normally as essential a part of the portative organ music as they were for singers and wind players, and the use of electric blowers, now common on reconstructed instruments, means that this natural phrasing is lost in many modern performances of early music. It will be observed that the portative in plate V is reversed; the bass notes are on the right and the treble on the left. These reversed keyboards are sufficiently common into the seventeenth century, as Jack Schuman has pointed out, that they cannot all be accidental or artists' errors. We must accept the fact that some people played keyboard instruments in what we consider to be the wrong way round.

Plate 25 is one of the earliest, perhaps the first illustration, to show the portative organ. It has been suggested by Farmer (*Organ of the Ancients*) and Perrot that the secrets of organ making were preserved in the Middle East during the Dark Ages; perhaps it was in this area also that the portative was invented and that this is yet another of the instruments that made their way into Europe from this source.

Both portatives and positives were commonly built with one or two bass pipes at the treble end and it seems almost certain that these were drone pipes; there was probably a small lever which could be locked down and which allowed one of these pipes to sound without requiring a finger to hold down a key. The pipes at either or both ends were often enclosed in a castle which, although both ornamental and functional to the extent that it helped to hold everything together, was later abandoned, probably simply to save weight.

Larger organs continued in use, but the paintings and carvings of this period show people rather than places, so that there is a lack of illustrations of church interiors in which they might be seen. We have written descriptions in plenty which tell us that a certain church, or several chapels within a church, had their organ or organs, but no pictures to show them and none of the descriptions are so detailed as to reveal what size they were or what their capabilities. We can assume that the same basic invention which allowed for the construction of the smaller instruments was applied to the larger also. This was the keyboard with spring-controlled or balanced keys which would return of their own accord to the closed position when released. The earlier instruments were played either by pushing down and pulling up a lever or, more usually, by pushing a rod in and pulling it out again. The Romans had used a spring-returned key, as the Aquincum organ shows us, but this device had been forgotten and was not reinvented until the thirteenth century. Without such keys, music could only move slowly and considerable skill

and attention would be needed to avoid jerks between notes as one key was closed and the next opened. With sprung or balanced keys, music could move more swiftly so that the organ became useful for secular music as well as for the slower-moving church chants, and players could play a melodic line with only one hand, thus making possible the portative organ. The layout of the keyboard may have been simpler than the modern, for some illustrations suggest that only one 'black' note was used, the B flat; other pictures, however, suggest that although the seventh was the only note normally changeable in any scale, from flat to natural, the organ was designed to play in more than one key by being equipped with a twelve note octave already arranged in the same way as that of today.

The Bagpipes

We have referred to drones, not only in connexion with the organ but also with the fiddle and the symphony. The instrument which we today associate invariably with drones is the bagpipe and it is interesting to note that in the earlier representations of this instrument no drone is apparent. The Roman origin of the bagpipe, which is frequently mentioned, is by no means certain and depends wholly upon literary references and upon the interpretation of the word *utricularis*, which may or may not have meant a bag in this sense. It has been suggested by Armstrong Davison that the first illustration of a bagpiper is the musician under King David's left foot on plate 8 and that the lump behind his right armpit is a small bag; there is no blowpipe visible, however, and it is difficult to see how the air was introduced into the bag, if that is what it is. It has also been suggested that the origin of the bagpipe was the bladder pipe (plates 26 and 27), pipes whose reeds were enclosed in a bladder instead of in the player's mouth. The evidence from non-European and from early European instruments, however, strongly suggests that the bagpipe was invented simply as a labour-saving device. Certainly by classical Greek times, and possibly much earlier, it was the custom for reed players to breathe in through their noses while blowing out through the mouth, using the cheeks as an auxiliary air reservoir, so as to obtain a continuous flow of sound. This trick of nose breathing is not difficult to acquire; the difficulty lies in avoiding an

Plate 26 Bladder pipes with short chanter and long drone. (Cantigas [*f 209.*] *Escorial J.b.2*)

Plate 27 Bladder pipes with curved bells. (Cantigas [*f 227.*] *Escorial J.b.2*)

alteration of pressure, and hence of pitch, when changing from diaphragm pressure to cheek pressure and back again. The use of a bag as an external reservoir makes playing such instruments far easier and avoids any risk of changes of pressure. That such bags were invented in the Middle East seems probable, for it is in that area that we still find instruments today which are played either directly by the mouth or through a bag and which have no difference between them save for the provision of a block to which the bag might be tied, the block which became the stock in which the pipes of the European bagpipe are set. A confirmation of this hypothesis of invention in the Middle East is provided by the bagpipes shown in the *Cantigas* on plates 28 and 29, which appear to be far more elaborate and far more fully developed instruments than those in contemporary sources from other parts of Europe, further from Middle Eastern influence.

The bagpipes in plate 28 are simple instruments, each with one chanter and no drone. Those in plate 29 are more complex and it is difficult to determine just how they were constructed. These pipes probably consist of a chanter behind and a drone pipe in front, the circles on the front pipe being decoration rather than finger holes, with the two pipes sharing a common stock. Another miniature in the same manuscript (folio 313v) shows an entirely different form of bagpipe, instantly recognisable as identical with the modern Italian zampogna, with two chanters and multiple drones, whose sound was imitated by Handel in the 'Pastoral Symphony' from the *Messiah*.

The bagpipes used in the rest of Europe at this period were much simpler instruments. Plate IV shows an instrument that is simply a shawm in a bag. Plate 33, at the top of the page, shows a bag with a cylindrical chanter, again without a drone. Plate V also shows shawms in a bag but now with a single drone, sometimes a long conical drone pipe, as in plate V where it is drawn as a trumpet, even to the banner hanging from it, and sometimes as a cylindrical drone pipe, as on the modern Highland instrument and many others. Plate 30 shows a more complex instrument, with several cylindrical drones sharing a stock with a conical chanter. The bagpipe which was to become the normal instrument of the Middle Ages in Europe was the bagged shawm, that

Plate 28 Bagpipes without drones. (Cantigas [*f 235v.*] *Escorial J.b.2*)

Plate 29 Bagpipes with chanter and drone in common stock. (Cantigas [*f 251v.*] *Escorial J.b.2*)

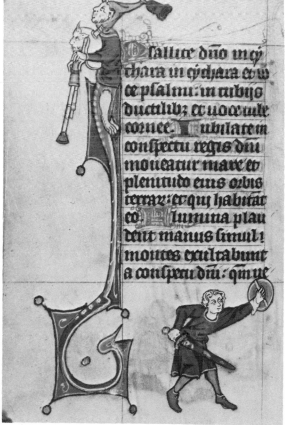

Plate 30 Bagpipe with conical chanter and two cylindrical drones in common stock; clapper bell on player's hood. (*British Library, Stowe 17* [*f 44v.*])

with the conical chanter and initially one cylindrical drone. This pipe is still to be found in Spain and in parts of France today.

The Shawm

The shawm itself also frequently appears (plates II, 9, 31 and 38). This instrument of conical bore played with a double reed is first found among the Faliscans, one of the Etruscan tribes, in the fourth century BC and was known in ancient Rome. It then seems to have vanished from the European scene and to have reappeared in the twelfth century from the Middle East. It was not only to Europe that it travelled; it was carried by Muslim traders and warriors throughout the known world, from India to Tibet, from China to Java and from southern Europe to Nigeria. There are two basic Arabic words for the shawm, *gaida* and *zurna* and these are the roots of the name for the shawm in almost all these areas. Our own shawm may come either from the Latin *calamis* or from the Arabic *zurna*; the Chinese *sona* and the Indian *shanai* are certainly from *zurna*. Our waits, the town bands who mostly played on shawms, along with the Spanish *gaita* and the Nigerian *alghaita* come from *gaida*.

The characteristic of the shawm is its loud sound which rings inside the ears. The player does not touch the reed with his lips but pouches it in his mouth, the lips being held either on the staple, the tube on which the reed is mounted, or on the lowest part of the reed just above the staple. The tips of the reed are thus free to vibrate with the maximum intensity, producing a sound very different from that of the oboe whose reed, although similar in pattern, is firmly gripped by the lips to control it and to produce the sound that we know today in our orchestras. Shawms can still be heard in folk music in Europe and elsewhere and in non-European art musics in a number of parts of the world. The shawm in plate 38, for example, which is playing for a procession dancing out of the gates of Constantinople, is still used in Turkey.

Other forms of reed pipe were used in the *Cantigas* but were less generally accepted for art music in the rest of Europe, although they were the prototypes of such instruments as the Welsh pibcorn (see plate 58) and the Scots stock and horn and led, eventually, to our clarinet.

Trumpets and Horns

The long trumpets, *al nafir* in Arabic and *añafil* in Spanish, appear also in the *Cantigas* (plate 32). These were the great instruments of state among the Moorish armies and became immediately popular in the European armies also; they can be seen in manuscripts from all over Europe from the middle of the thirteenth century onwards. Their use was by no means confined to Europe and the Middle East. Their place of origin would seem to be in Central Asia and they spread thence in both directions: eastwards to Tibet, India and China and westwards to the Middle East and thence to North Africa, Europe and West Africa, in all of which areas they are still in use. In Europe, the añafil often carried a banner emblazoned with the arms of the owner, one advantage of which is that it has often enabled scholars to determine for whom a manuscript was illuminated. In plate 32 this banner is small and triangular and hangs from one of the decorative bosses whose function is to strengthen the metal at the end of a section of tubing. The long trumpet was never made in one piece but always in short joints which fit into each other; these may have been made as a push fit, so that the instrument would come apart for storage, or they may have been soldered together; in either case, the boss is a useful strengthening device (plates 33 and 36). The banner later became square or rectangular and was usually attached to the end of the bell and to the boss nearest to the bell, as in plates IV and 38. The trumpet was mainly a military instrument and seems to have been used without any restrictions; it was not until the end of the Middle Ages that it became so closely associated with royalty that its use was forbidden to lesser persons over much of Europe. A common name for it was buisine, from the Latin *bucina*, a word which in German eventually became *posaun*, the modern name for the trombone; we shall trace the changes which made this use of the name appropriate in the next chapter.

The only other instrument of the trumpet family to appear with any frequency in the illustrations of this period is the hunting horn, which was already known as the bugle (Latin, *bucullus*, a small ox), since it was originally made from an ox horn. It was a normal part of hunting costume and can be seen

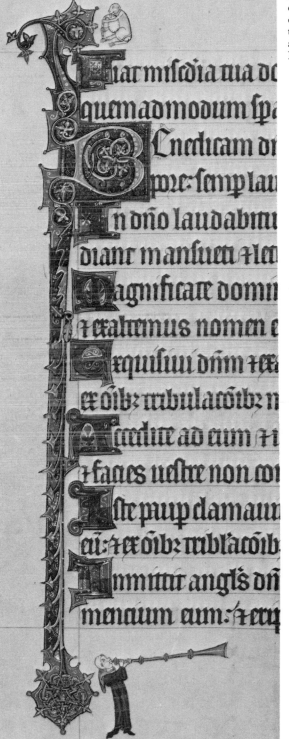

Plate 33   Monkey playing droneless bagpipe with cylindrical chanter and man playing long trumpet with four triple bosses and wide bell. (The Gorleston Psalter [*f 43v.*])

Plate 34 Long horns with finger holes. (Cantigas [*f 243v.*] *Escorial J.b.2*)

Plate V Psalm 100. Pair of hand bells, portative organ with drone pipes at treble end and reversed keyboard, bagpipe with conical chanter and trumpet drone, symphony, nakers. (The Luttrell Psalter [*f 176*] *British Library, Add 42130*) East Anglian, *c.* 1340

Plate 35 Transverse flutes, both blown left-handed. (Cantigas [*f 218v.*] *Escorial J.b.2*)

hanging from a belt or from a shoulder strap in many pictures. The finger-hole horn is seldom seen in the thirteenth and fourteenth centuries, although two large examples appear in the *Cantigas* (plate 34).

The Flute

The transverse flute, a cylindrical tube with six finger holes and with an embouchure or mouth hole in the side of the tube near the closed end, was occasionally used at this period, as in plate 35 in which both players are playing left-handed, but more frequently we encounter the flute played via a duct, like our recorder. Multiple instruments, such as the triple duct flute shown in plate 8 under King David's right foot, were not uncommon, though double flutes are more usual than triple; the third tube on this instrument appears to be a drone pipe. The pipes are almost always parallel tubes and are quite different from the double duct flutes of the late Middle Ages and the Renaissance which appear quite often in Italian paintings as two divergent tubes both with six or more finger holes. These are misinterpretations of the ancient Greek aulos which was already mistakenly thought of as a flute and not as the reed-blown instrument it really was. This is one example

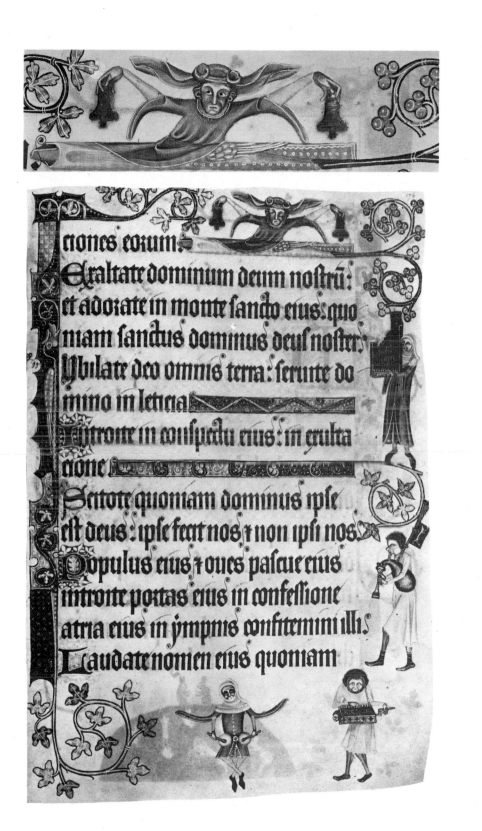

ctiones eorum.

Exaltate dominum deum nostrū: et adorate in monte sancto eius: quoniam sanctus dominus deus noster.

Jubilate deo omnis terra: seruite domino in leticia.

Intronte in conspectu eius: in exulta cione.

Scitote quoniam dominus ipse est deus: ipse fecit nos, t non ipsi nos.

Populus eius t oues pascue eius introite portas eius in confessione atria eius in ympnis confitemini illi.

Laudate nomen eius quoniam

of the care that must be taken when dealing with instruments from illustrations in which some instruments are used symbolically rather than factually. Single duct flutes, the ancestors of the recorder, appear occasionally at this period, usually associated with shepherds who still play such flutes in many parts of Europe today, but sometimes with grotesques, as in plate 36, or with ordinary people.

Pipe and Tabor

By far the commonest duct flute was the tabor pipe (plates IV, 37, 38, 39). This was a flute with three finger holes which was played with one hand. The other hand held the beater for a drum which was strapped to the shoulder or to the upper part of the arm that held the pipe. The pipe and tabor was the basic dance band from the thirteenth century onwards and survived among folk players up to the end of the nineteenth century in Britain and continues in use in other parts of Europe and in Latin America, where it was introduced by the Spanish Conquistadors. Although the pipe has only three holes, two for the fingers in the front and one at the back for the thumb, these are near the lower end of the pipe, rather than in the middle as on some earlier instruments, and make it possible for the pipe to sound all the notes of the diatonic scale, and a few chromatic notes as well, by utilising the upper harmonics of the pipe. The pipe is narrower than a recorder in bore, thus making it easy to overblow, and the lowest note that is used is the octave above the fundamental, the first overblown note. Three finger holes suffice to fill all the gaps between that note and the harmonics above; see p. 76 for the notes of the harmonic series.

Percussion Instruments

The tabor at this period was a small cylindrical drum with a snare, a strand of gut, running across

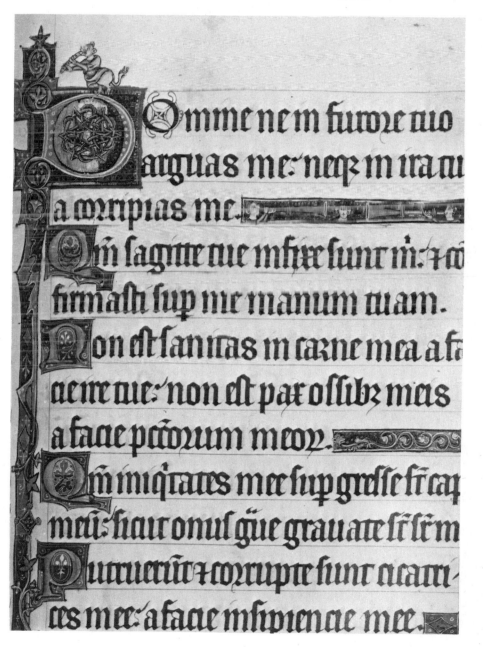

Plate 37 Pipe and tabor players. (Cantigas [*f 333.*] *Escorial J.b.2*)

Plate 38 Party dancing out of Constantinople. Two long trumpets with banners, dancing shawm player, dancing pipe and tabor player. (The Luttrell Psalter [*f 164v.*] *British Library, Add 42130*) East Anglia, *c.* 1340

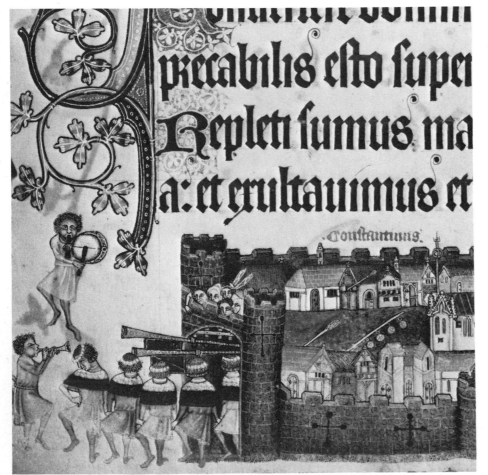

the struck head to add a buzz or rattle to the sound. Judging from the very few pictures or carvings which show a tabor from the back, there may also have been a snare on the lower head as well, as we have it on the side drum today. As can be seen in plate 39, the tabor was tensioned with V's of rope running from head to head, as on the modern military drum. Sliding buffs of cord or leather are pulled down these V's from their points, so drawing the ropes of the V together and tightening them and thus tightening the drum heads. There is no definite evidence as to what sort of music was played on the pipe and tabor, save that it was almost invariably dance music, but, as I have discussed in detail elsewhere, it is probable that the tabor rhythms were simple and steadily repetitive as they certainly were in the late sixteenth century and as they are in many parts of Europe today.

The timbre, the ancestor of the Jacobean timbrel and of our tambourine, was one of the commonest drums in the thirteenth and fourteenth centuries and is yet another instrument which we acquired from the Middle East. It was made from a circular wooden frame, like a riddle or sieve, with a skin across one side and with small metal cymbals let into the frame to produce a jingling rattle (plate II). It was the timbre, rather than any other type of drum, which was almost invariably portrayed in bibles and psalters to represent the word *tympanum* in the Latin text. It is one of the puzzles of musical history that so popular a drum should have fallen out of use in the later Renaissance, surviving as a folk instrument in southern Europe, North Africa and the Middle East, until it was recalled into the orchestra by the Romantic composers of the late nineteenth century to add local colour to their Spanish or Arabian impressions. It will be noticed that the plate shows a snare running across the head; this was a less common feature of the timbre than of other drums.

The nakers were widely used in the Middle Ages: a pair of small kettledrums suspended from the player's waist, as in plate V. They also were imported from the Middle East, the Arabic *naqara* becoming nakers in English and similar names in other European languages. The illustrations of both nakers and timbre suggest that they were used in all sorts of music and not only for dance music. The nakers reached Britain later than the timbre, first appearing

Plate 39 Pipe & tabor. *c.* 1270.
(*Lincoln Cathedral Angel Choir,
S 8.*)

Plate 40   Bell-chime in a case.
(Cantigas [ƒ 359.] Escorial J.b.2)

in literature in 1300 and in art in 1340, but they were known in France certainly by 1280 and possibly earlier. They were played with heavy beaters, shaped like miniature clubs. Regrettably, we have no evidence at all as to the sort of music played on them, nor of what, if any, difference there was between the sounds of the two drums. They continued in use into the fifteenth century and their name continues in modern times in a slang usage which derives from their appearance.

The other percussion instruments which were used included the cymbals, the cymbala by which the medieval writers normally meant sets of chime bells rather than cymbals, the pellet bells such as were used on animal trappings and jesters' costumes and the triangle. By far the most important of these were the bells. These had four functions: firstly they could be attached to costumes or to animals, either to make a pleasant clangour (plate 30), as an aid to location or to frighten away evil spirits as in later folk uses; secondly they could be played to add a joyful noise to whatever else was going on, as in plate V, a typical example of a pair of handbells being used as simple noise makers, for two bells cannot give any musically logical choice of pitch; thirdly they could be installed in church towers and other buildings, and fourthly they could be fitted up as a chime of bells on which a full musical part could be played. This last use was very common in churches, often associated with the organ, as many literary descriptions reveal. Sets of bells were often connected with King David (plate 8) and also appear in other similar settings (plate IV). Their musical use is not always easy to determine, for illustrations showing a full set of bells, as in plate 8, are unusual, and more frequently one finds smaller numbers, as in plate IV, leaving one to wonder whether the artist was saving space or whether sets of bells were often without all the notes of the gamut. A single octave would suffice for any piece of music because, since most people find it difficult to determine in which octave a bell is sounding, pitches beyond the range could be brought into the octave; however, most pictures show fewer than the seven bells necessary for this. An instrument unique, so far as we know, in its period and for several centuries thereafter may be seen in plate 40. This appears to be a form of carillon, a set of bells played by remote control. The later Flemish carillons were played via long tracker wires from a keyboard (plate 84); the instrument in plate 40 has a series of levers protruding from its box and it requires only the wires and the keyboard to convert it into a carillon, something, combined with the later Spanish domination of the Netherlands, that makes one wonder whether perhaps this Hispano-Moorish instrument was the source of the carillon.

The triangle makes its first appearance at this time, sometimes as a plain three-sided or trapezoidal instrument, but more often with rings on the horizontal bar. These rings prolong the sound into a buzzing jingle quite different from the ting that we hear today. Both triangular and trapezoidal forms survived into the fifteenth and sixteenth centuries as can be seen from plates VII and 83. The triangular shape has continued into modern use, but the rings vanished in the early nineteenth century.

We have already encountered the use of small cymbals mounted upon the ends of tongs. The larger instruments, held in the hands, appear in both the *Cantigas* manuscripts (plate 41). Both manuscripts show the cymbals held vertically and struck together horizontally, as we play them today, unlike most medieval and renaissance illustrations, in which they are held horizontally and struck vertically. All medieval and renaissance sources show cymbals made of thick metal and with high domes. Such instruments must produce sounds of definite pitch, unlike our modern cymbals, and the fact that those in the *Cantigas* are tied together with cord suggests that they were matched in pitch and tied together, as in the East today, so that pairs would not become confused. It is difficult for us to conceive how they were used, for to our way of thinking the sound would be an obtrusive high drone which might not, unless the player carried a whole stock of pairs of cymbals with him, be suitable to the key of the music. Unfortunately, the use of percussion instruments at this period is the subject that we know the least about; we see them being played in the pictures but we have no certain idea of their sound nor any specific music for them. Such information as is available will be found in James Blades's and my books listed in the bibliography.

Plate 41   Pairs of cymbals.
(*Cantigas* [*f 176v*] *Escorial J.b.2*)

The Use of the Instruments

We have now described all the instruments commonly encountered at this period but we have said little of their use or of the music played upon them. This is almost inevitable, for practically none of the music was written for specific forces. A three-part piece of music, for example one of Adam de la Halle's rondeaux, might have words laid beneath one or two of the lines, leaving us to assume that those parts were sung and the third played on an instrument. Perhaps this was so; perhaps only one line was sung and two were instrumental; perhaps all three lines were sung and may have been sung unaccompanied or doubled with instruments. Or there may have been no voices and all three lines played on instruments, or two lines played and one omitted. All these are possible, and indeed are likely, for performances were never fixed in the way that they are today. Far more music existed than has survived and even more was improvised and never written down. Scholars today disagree about the interpretation of what little has come down to us; they argue about which rhythmic mode a piece should be in; whether it should be in triple or duple time for instance, in 6/8 or 2/4. There is dispute about musica ficta, whether leading notes, the B in the key of C, were flats or naturals, and about many other details, further information on which can be found in such studies as those by Gustave Reese and in the *New Oxford History of Music*. With so little known about the music, it is not surprising that less is known about what the instruments played. We know that drones were often used to support the melody; we know that percussion instruments provided a rhythmic accompaniment to dance and other music; we know that an established melodic line could be accompanied by other improvised lines. We know that some instruments were regarded as more suitable than others for some purposes; that dance music for instance, while it could be played on any instruments, was usually played on pipe and tabor or fiddle, psaltery, gittern or citole. Other instruments were more suited to church music, such as the organ and the bells, and these must have doubled the vocal lines in the hymns and other music which was inserted into the basic material of the Mass. It has been suggested that because many popes and bishops inveighed against the use of instruments in church, they were obeyed and instruments were not used. However, it does not seem likely that such prohibitions were merely cautionary; they must have been against something that was actually happening. The use of instruments was forbidden because, and not in case, the clergy were using instruments, and the prohibitions had to be repeated again and again because, after a few years, the instruments crept back into use. We can therefore assume that bells and organs were not the only instruments to be heard in church services and that from time to time the fiddles, psalteries, lutes and gitterns and all the other instruments that we see used by celestial choirs were used by earthly choirs also.

The tuning of the string instruments was fairly arbitrary; each player selected the intervals between strings that he preferred. The written descriptions indicate that the instruments with three or four strings were tuned in fifths or fourths, for these are the intervals that can lie best under a player's hand. With three fingers used to stop the strings, a fifth is the obvious interval: C on the open string, D for the forefinger, E for the middle finger, F for the ring finger and G either for the little finger or on the next open string. For a heavier instrument that needs more of the hand to support its weight, or for a larger one on which only alternate fingers can reach the correction positions, a fourth is the more appropriate: C on the open string, D for the forefinger again since the hand can be set higher up the neck, E for the ring finger and F on the next string. On those instruments which had five or more strings, one or more strings were probably drones, to be struck with the bow on each up or down bow or, if the bridge were flat enough, to be sustained throughout. Where, as in some illustrations, one string runs beside the neck of the fiddle instead of above it, as it does on the later lira da braccio (plate 86), it may be assumed that the player plucked that string with his thumb as a rhythmic drone, a technique which John Sothcott has revived today with great effect.

The psalteries, harps and other instruments with a string for each note, and sometimes the organs, were tuned diatonically to any key which was convenient. That is to say, if the key were C, only the white notes of the piano were used, with the exception of the seventh note of the scale which was often present both as a B flat and as a B natural. There was no modulation or changing of key in this music, nor was there any feeling that any piece should be played in a particular key; the player chose the key that best suited himself, his instrument or the voice of the singer that he was accompanying, and tuned accordingly. All these instruments may have been used to accompany a singer; the only instruments for which this would have been inappropriate are the symphony, the bells, the pipe and tabor, the shawm and, of course, the trumpet and the horn. Those used most often for accompanying a single voice were the harp and the portative organ; the minstrel could accompany himself upon either without interfering with his singing, something that could hardly be done so easily with a fiddle, for instance.

The horn with finger holes was on equal terms with any other melody instrument, but the ordinary short horn could produce only one note which, as on the modern English hunting horn, could be lipped up and down somewhat; it could be blown in rhythmic patterns to fit a simple code of signals. The long trumpets could produce the pitches we think of as bugle calls, the first half dozen of the harmonic series (p. 76), which could also be rhythmically varied. If the trumpet were made in such a length that its basic pitch matched the key in which other instruments were playing, it could produce common chord fanfares in concert with them. It is generally assumed that the trumpet was solely a military instrument, but its presence with other instruments in plate IV and other sources suggests that such fanfares and flourishes may have been heard in medieval music.

On the whole, however, instruments were already divided into two groups that lasted through the Renaissance: the *instruments hauts* and the *instruments bas*, the loud and the soft, and, with the exception of the percussion and the later sackbut and cornett, these groups seldom or never mixed. The reed instruments and the duct flutes, in particular, work only at a set air pressure and, if blown harder, play sharper as well as louder; blown more gently, they play flat as well as softly. They were therefore placed in whichever group was appropriate. Once the loud group was established, quieter instruments such as fiddles had perforce to be placed in the soft group, simply because they would not be audible in the loud. The groups were also divided in their use. The loud instruments were more often employed out of doors and the soft for more intimate and domestic music. The pride of place in the loud instruments was taken by the shawms. These were instruments for street music, dance and processional music and were used for any ceremonial or joyous occasion. They were used by the town watchmen in their rounds, hence the use of the term waits for such a band of watchmen, and would only appear indoors for dancing or for processions in a large building such as a church. The bagpipe could be used either for loud or for soft music, depending upon the type of instrument blown through the bag; a bagpipe with a shawm chanter would be used in the same way as a shawm, but there is much evidence, in the later periods at least, that quiet bagpipes were used for indoor music.

The instruments of the central Middle Ages were thus mainly those imported from non-European sources. In the later Middle Ages, they were adapted and modified to such an extent that they became clearly and recognisably European and wholly distinct from their Moorish origins.

Chapter 3
The Hundred Years War

The Black Death to the Fall of Constantinople, 1348–1453

While the church and, to a lesser extent, the aristocracy remained the great patrons of musicians and artists, it was in this period that the middle classes, the bourgeoisie, began to grow into importance. The prosperous wool merchants of England who built so many great churches, the traders and merchants of the Hanseatic League and of the Italian city-states wished to perform and to hear music just as much as the princes and the bishops of the courtly establishments. Some were content with the simpler songs and dances which were not unlike those of the earlier period; others preferred the more solemn, more elaborate music of Dunstable and Dufay. This dichotomy is visible also in the representations of instruments. Sometimes we find, as often on the misericords and other church carvings, instruments that differ little from those that we have already encountered. Sometimes we find instruments which are far more advanced, such as the Dordrecht recorder (plate 57) and, above all, we find the development of a whole new group of instruments, the string keyboards.

Keyboard Instruments

The Clavichord

In the previous period, the only instruments on which it was possible to play more than one part at a time were the large and the positive organs. Such organs were normally church instruments and, for domestic purposes, other instruments were required, instruments of a type which would not require a team of assistants to pump bellows before they could be played. The first of these was the clavichord. We have already encountered the monochord, an instrument used for the measurement of intervals and for teaching choirs to sing, with two fixed bridges and a sliding bridge which was moved along the soundboard to positions marked upon it, according to the pitches required. Sliding the bridge took time and looking for the correct mark was a nuisance. The logical development can be seen in a drawing from a comparatively late manuscript of about 1475 (plate 42), which describes and embodies the earlier teachings of Johannes Gallicus on music. This shows

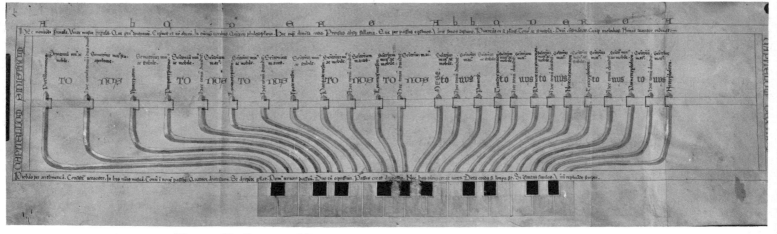

Plate 42   The first stage of the conversion of the monochord into the clavichord. Italian, 15th century. (*Joannis Gallici*, Liber Notabilis Musicae [*f 15.*] *British Library, Add 22315*)

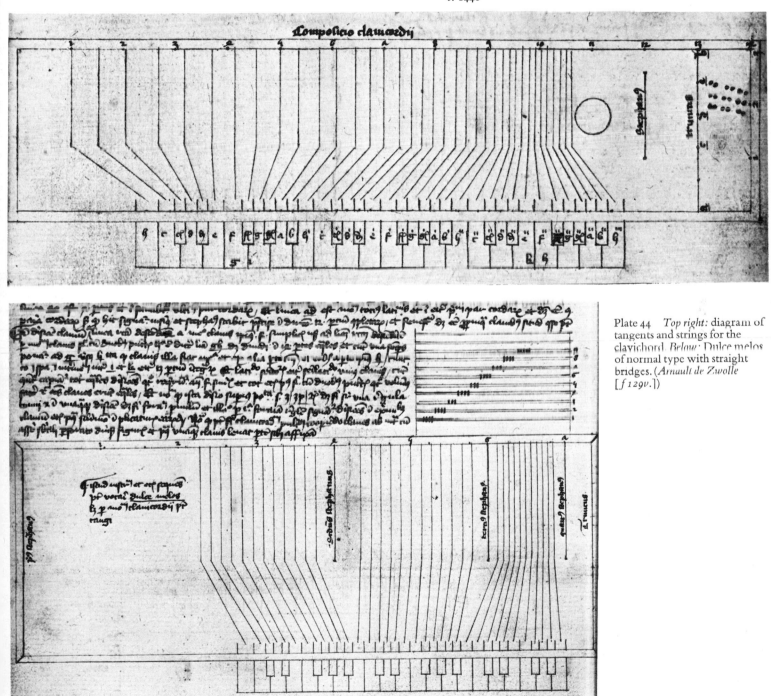

Plate 43   Clavichord with nine pairs of strings for thirty-seven keys. (*Henri Arnault de Zwolle, Traités [f 129] Bibliothèque Nationale, Paris, latin 7295*) *c.* 1440

Plate 44   *Top right:* diagram of tangents and strings for the clavichord. *Below:* Dulce melos of normal type with straight bridges. (*Arnault de Zwolle [f 129v.]*)

a monochord provided with a keyboard. On the inner end of each key is a tangent, a small blade of metal, which, when the key is depressed, rises and touches the string. Because the shanks of the keys are bent, the tangents touch the string at the correct points for each note of the keyboard. The touch of the tangent is sufficient to set the string in vibration and, so long as the tangent remains in contact with the string, only the portion of the string to the right of the tangent will sound, since the extreme left-hand end of the string is deadened by a strip of felt which is not shown in the drawing. The invention of the keyboard and tangent allowed players to use the monochord melodically but it was not, of course, possible to play more than one note at a time. This restriction was overcome by fitting a few more strings, as in plate 45 (the right-hand large light), one of the earliest illustrations, which has six strings played from a keyboard with all the keys in one line, without sharps and flats. We do not know whether this is artist's licence or whether such a keyboard existed. There appear to be twenty-six keys, which would allow for two chromatic octaves or for three and a half diatonic octaves. In this stained glass window, which was painted in about 1440, and for which the contractor, John Prudde, agreed to paint from models supplied to him, presumably from Warwick, we can see the bridge under all the strings on the player's right and the felt listing, which prevented the left-hand part of the string from sounding, in three rows to the left.

We can be fairly sure that the clavichord, or monacordys as it was then known—another indication of its derivation from the monochord—was by no means new in 1440 from the almost exactly contemporary working drawings of Henri Arnault de Zwolle (plates 43 and 44). There are a number of medieval and renaissance writers to whom all historians of musical instruments owe an incalculable debt. Some, such as Johannes Tinctoris, left us only descriptions. Others, such as Sebastian Virdung, Martin Agricola, Michael Praetorius and Marin Mersenne, provided drawings as well, which greatly increase the value of their work, for illustrations tell us, far better than written descriptions, the extent to which instruments altered from the time of one author to that of the next. In addition, they often reveal details which the author did not bother to

describe in the text, either because they were not of sufficient importance to him or because they were too well known to his contemporaries to need description. One of the most important of these authors, and one of the least known because he wrote before the invention of printing, was Arnault de Zwolle. The value of his work is enormously increased by the care with which he drew his illustrations, using compass and rule and showing not only the external features of the instruments but also mechanical and constructional details, sufficiently accurately that it has been possible to reconstruct a number of his instruments.

Arnault's clavichord (plate 43) has a keyboard of the pattern which we still use today: running from B in the bass to C in the treble, it shows the seven 'white' and five 'black' notes in each octave that have been used ever since. There were nine double strings, the tuning pins for which can be seen in three rows at the right-hand end of the instrument. There is a single bridge, just opposite the 12 mark, and a round sound hole opposite the 11. The way that the strings were shared among the tangents can be seen in the upper, grid-like part of plate 44, the first (lowest in the drawing) string being used for B, C, C sharp and D, and so on until we arrive at the last string which should produce the top G, G sharp, A, B flat and B, but, as Edwin Ripin has pointed out in the *Musical Quarterly*, the number of tangents and the number of keys in the drawings do not correspond. All the strings were tuned to the same pitch and these early clavichords differed from the monochord of plate 42 solely in the fact that, with more than one string, it was possible to play more than one note at a time, provided that no chord smaller than a third was used.

The clavichord survived long after the pianoforte had totally replaced the harpsichord, because of its unique mechanism. It was, and it remains, the only keyboard instrument on which the player is in total control of the sound for the whole time that it lasts. On the piano and on the harpsichord, the player controls the way in which the sound is begun by his touch on the key and he can terminate the sound by releasing the key or the sustaining pedal and so damping the string, but he can do little or nothing to affect the quality of the sound during its duration. On the organ, he can do very little to control the

beginning of the sound, due to the mechanism between his finger and the opening at the foot of the pipe; he can control the length of the note by keeping a finger on the key and, on the later organs, he can increase or decrease the loudness by opening or closing panels which surround the swell box or, on modern electronic instruments, by the use of a volume control. Only on the clavichord can a player control the beginning of a note by his touch on the key and control its loudness during its duration by a vertical vibrato, the *bebung*, of his finger on the key. In addition, because his finger is on one end of the key and the tangent on the other end is in contact with the string throughout the duration of the note, there is an immediacy of contact, a feeling that one is in complete control of the sound, that can be experienced on no other keyboard instrument. Immediately the finger releases the key, the tangent leaves the string and the vibration, and hence the sound, is stifled by the listing, the felt wound over the left-hand end. The clavichord has the additional advantage that its sound is very quiet, making the player conscious of an intimacy with his instrument and avoiding disturbance or nuisance for others, for the clavichord has been described as the only instrument on which one occupant of a double bed could play in the still watches of the night without disturbing the other. As a result, the clavichord throughout its history has not only been a favourite instrument in its own right but has also been the ideal practice instrument for the players of other, larger and louder, keyboard instruments. In the eighteenth century, all organists had clavichords at home on which they could practise and well into the nineteenth century virtuoso pianists on tour carried a clavichord in preference to a dumb keyboard.

The Chekker

Arnault illustrates and describes also the harpsichord (plate 48), showing not only the lay-out of the instrument but also giving detail drawings of three different types of jack mechanism for plucking the strings. The fourth mechanism, that in the top right-hand corner, is different. This is a form of hammer mechanism with which the string is struck when the hammer is flipped up by the key, instead of being plucked by a quill. This mechanism could be

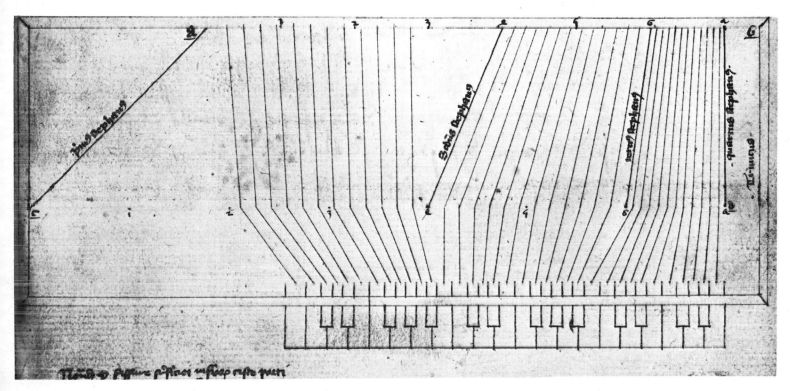

applied either to a harpsichord or to a clavichord or to a different instrument, the dulce melos. Arnault says that all these instruments would then sound like the dulce melos. He is here describing a type of piano, in either grand or square shape, nearly three centuries before Cristofori reinvented it.

Arnault describes three types of dulce melos. The first, which he mentions only briefly, is a village instrument, either a dulcimer or a string drum such as the tambourin de Béarn or tsountsounia. The second, the normal design (plate 44), has a keyboard like that of the clavichord but with a series of bridges, named as *stephanos* in the drawings, under the strings to divide them into aliquot parts. With twelve strings, each tuned to a different fundamental semitone, from the left-hand bridge to the next provides the basic octave; from the second bridge to the third gives the next octave and from the third bridge to the fourth the highest. The third model (plate 46), he says is the best because the sloping

bridges allow the strings to be more accurately divided. Arnault says, further, that the hammers of the dulce melos may be replaced by normal harpsichord jacks, thus describing the virginals, an instrument which is normally thought of as originating in the sixteenth century.

Canon Galpin identified the dulce melos with the chekker, an instrument which is known from many references in the fourteenth and fifteenth centuries but no example of which has survived. The French name for the instrument was *échiquier* or *eschaquiel* and there have been attempts to derive these names from a resemblance between the row of hammers and chess pieces, the French for chess being *échecs*, and to derive from the instrument the word jack, the name for the device which carries the quill to pluck the string of the harpsichord. It seems probable that Galpin was right and that Arnault's description and drawings are all that survives of this mystery instrument, a favourite of kings and of princes.

The Harpsichord

The harpsichord, unlike the chekker and the clavichord, is played by plucking the strings and it has usually been supposed that it was invented as a mechanised psaltery. As can be seen in plates 45, upper right, and 47, the right-hand large light, the two instruments are not unlike in shape and, in this example at least, in size, although the psaltery was not usually as big as it is shown in these windows. The iconographic evidence leaves no doubt at all that the earliest harpsichords were the full-size instruments, in what we would think of as grand piano shape, and that the smaller patterns, such as virginals and spinets, were a later development. Arnault's illustration (plate 48), one of the earliest known, shows a full-size, single manual harpsichord with a single rank of strings, one string for each note; the drawing shows only two strings but it is clear from their position on the sound board bridge, near the tail of the instrument, that one is shorter than the other and that they produced two different pitches. These strings were plucked by a quill mounted in a jack which was thrown up to the string from the inner or tail end of the key. Arnault gives three designs of jack, the left-hand one in the picture, which is shown both from the front and from the back, being the one he considered to be the best. This jack is shown on its side, the quill set in its hinged tongue being at the top of the drawing and more easily seen in the lower drawing. The jack pivots on a wire which runs the width of the instrument and which fits into the hook in the tail of the jack. Arnault says that the quill was usually of metal, although he does mention feather, which became the normal material in the following period.

The harpsichord in the Beauchamp windows (plate 45) raises one major question. The keyboard seems, like that of the clavichord in the neighbouring light, to have a straight row of keys without 'black' notes, but there appear to be two such rows. Is it possible that the double manual harpsichord was known as early as this? One can only say that it is possible although unlikely. If it were a double manual it would probably be a transposing double, like those to be described in the next chapter, rather than a contrasting double such as we are accustomed to from the baroque instruments. Transposing key-

Plate 47 *Left to right:* pipe and tabor, angel with pipe and another with tabor, two rebecs with saw-edge bows, psaltery, (censer), positive organ. (*The Beauchamp Chapel, east half of the south window*)

Plate 48   Harpsichord with
(*above right*) four types of jack:
two views (*left*) of the best type
and (*extreme right*) the hammer for
the dulce melos. (*Arnault de
Zwolle* [*f 128.*])

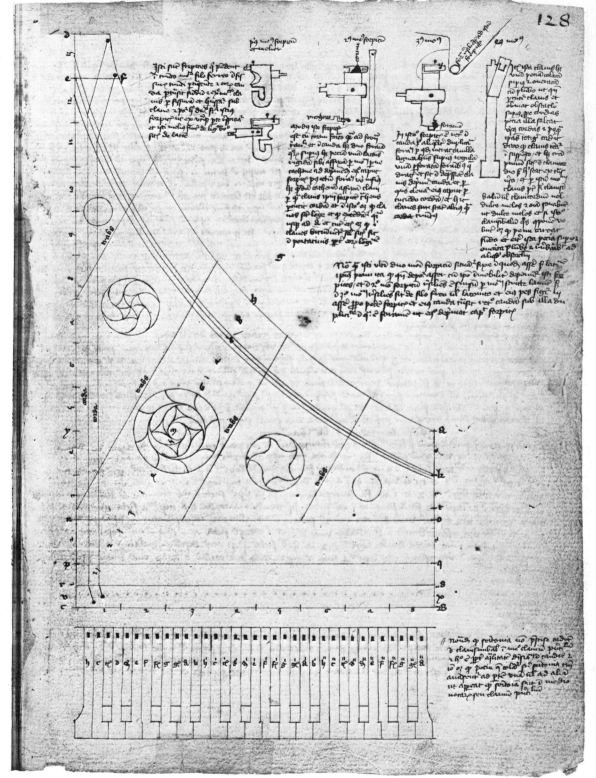

boards could have been of use at any period, so that it is not impossible that the glass painter should have had such an instrument before him. There are no other details of the instrument visible in the glass, save that ornamental designs were already applied to the outside of the case. Arnault's drawing is much more detailed; he shows not only the five sound holes, three of them filled with traceried roses, but draws also the positions of the bridge and of the four bars glued to the underside of the sound board.

The Organ

The small portative still existed and continued with little change (plates VII, 54 upper right quarter and 58), though Arnault de Zwolle drew two separate plans for the lay-out of its pipes, one, the conventional pattern, with the largest pipes at the left, the other, which is occasionally illustrated elsewhere, with the longest pipes in the centre. As can be seen in plate 47, top right, the positive had

Plate 50   Front pipes of an organ
with keyboard, trackers and
roller boards. (*Arnault de Zwolle*
[*f131.*])

grown considerably and now sometimes had two manuals which, unlike those of the harpsichord, were almost certainly contrasting; they controlled different ranks of pipes so that the player could produce music of differing sonorities. This instrument is so much larger than the positives of the preceding and the succeeding centuries (plate 61) that one might doubt its portability were it not for the massive handle visible on the front below the keyboard with which, along with another at the back of the instrument, it could be carried around. Another positive, and one painted in the most perfect detail, is that of the famous Ghent altar-piece painted by the brothers van Eyck. This has a single keyboard but two ranks of pipes, the second being controlled by a stop lever to the left of the keyboard which is depressed when required and held down by a swinging latch, much like the old-fashioned swinging cover to a key-hole on a door. The slightly later large organ in plate 99 has similar stops and latches.

Larger organs, built into the church, were also in use (plate 49 in the gallery and plate 50). In plate 50, Arnault de Zwolle shows the lay-out for the façade of an organ. His descriptions are detailed, covering the design and construction of pipes of different types and of the bellows and other details, as well as describing the various mixtures and types of pipes used in an organ. It is clear that not only were some ranks of pipes used together with other ranks, sounding simultaneously as a mixture, but that the organist could draw on different ranks to obtain different sonorities. This was made possible by the re-invention of the stop, a device which had been known to the Romans and was fitted to the Aquincum organ. The stops are connected by levers to sliders, none of which are shown in Arnault's drawing, which allow the air access to each rank of pipes. By their use the organist can control the number of ranks sounding, admitting air to one, to all or to any combination of ranks. The drawing shows only the front rank, that which would be visible to the public, with the keyboard and the trackers which run from the keys to the roller boards and from the roller boards to the foot of each pipe. A façade balanced to make a pattern pleasing to the eye can only be built with roller boards; without them, each pipe must be set vertically above its key as on the portative and the smaller positive organs.

String Instruments

The Lute

Arnault also illustrates the lute (plate 51). He gives the whole geometric pattern of lute construction, spoiled only by having to reduce the length of the neck because the sheet of paper was too small. His apologetic description states that the neck should be as long as the width of the belly. He shows the barring below the belly (marked 'pons') and, in two drawings at the sides, gives a cross-section of the back, on the left, showing the separate staves from which it is made up, and a schema for the mould, on the right, on which the back is formed. This pattern of lute was widely used in its day, as many pictures show and has been copied today, most notably by Ian Harwood who has published details of his reconstruction. Not until nearly a century later did Laux Maler (plate XIII) produce a design which was radically different and which was the prototype from which later lutes took their pattern. That the lute was still a monophonic instrument, played with a quill plectrum, can be seen in plate 55, third large light from the left. The smaller lutes, the mandores in the next light, were also played with plectra, as was the citole, the similar instrument with a flat back, which can be seen in plate 54, upper left quarter.

The Psaltery and Dulcimer

The psaltery (plate VI, VII, 54 lower left quarter and 47 right-hand large light) was now firmly established in the pig's head shape. It was normally played with a quill plectrum in each hand but Arnault's description of the simplest dulce melos indicates that the dulcimer, the hammered psaltery whose strings were struck with two light beaters, was coming into use. The Italian name for this instrument, *salterio tedesco*, suggests that this manner of playing originated in Germany. The two instruments, psaltery and dulcimer, were much the same in appearance, save for differences in their bridging and stringing. When plucking with quills, the strings can all be in the same plane, running flat from bridge to bridge, because the player can dip the plectrum between them. When struck with hammers, however, there must be sufficient space to avoid hitting a neighbouring string. The dulcimer therefore had higher bridges than the psaltery and these were

Plate 51 Lute with (*left*) a section of the back and (*right*) the schema for the mould on which the back is formed. (*Arnault de Zwolle* [*f 132.*])

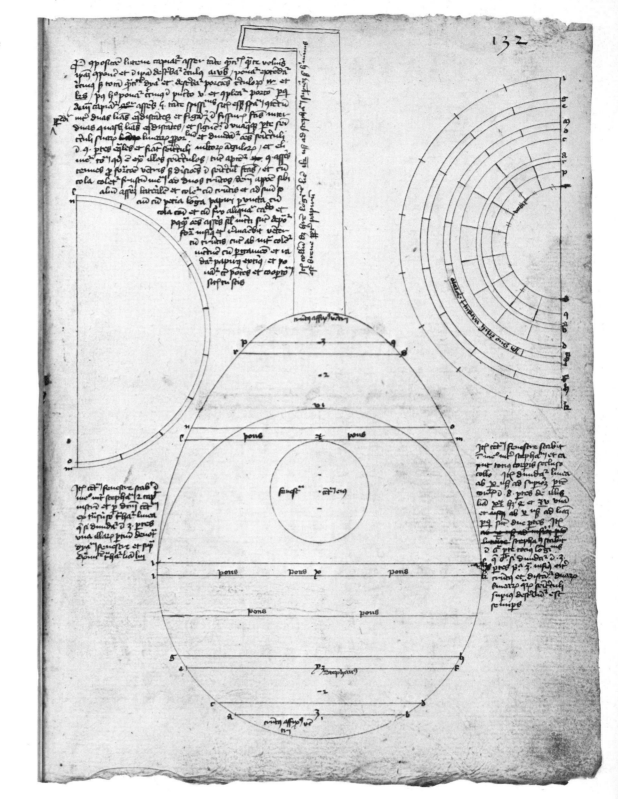

Plate 52 Irish harp. 14th century. (*Trinity College, Dublin*)

Plate 53   Adoration of the
Virgin. Eight-stringed harp and
three-stringed square fiddle.
(The Bedford Hours [ƒ 150v.])

Plate 54   *Lower left:* psaltery and
trumpet; *upper left*: rebec, lute,
citole, oval fiddle; *upper right*:
harp, portative organ, wind
instrument; *lower right*: small
cymbals, rotta. *c.* 1370.
(*Westminster Abbey, The Chapter
House*)

either individual bridges, like chess pawns, one for each string, or were a continuous arcaded bridge so that strings could alternately run over and under the bridge. Alternate strings were raised at the left or the right side of the instrument in order to provide clearance for the beaters. The psaltery was normally single strung, with one wire for each note, whereas the dulcimer usually had multiple courses with two, three or four wires for each note.

The Harp

The harp had changed but little since the earlier period. The same two basic types still existed, both the lighter instrument (which can be seen in plates VI, VII, 54 upper right quarter, 53 and 55 left-hand large light), sometimes with the brays in the belly, and the heavy Irish instrument which we have already encountered at Lincoln (plate 22) and of which we now have a surviving example, the Trinity College harp (plate 52) dating from the fourteenth century. This was strung with brass wire and was played with the finger-nails, producing, as Joan Rimmer who supervised its recent restoration says, a sound which is extraordinarily sweet and clear with a quality which is somewhat bell-like but with an added richness akin to that of a guitar. The harp was still a diatonic instrument, playing in whatever key the harper had tuned it to.

Fiddle, Rebec and Rotta

The fiddle still appears in a range of shapes (plates VI, VII, 54 upper left quarter and 53). Two other forms of bowed string instrument reappear in this period. The rebec, which had almost seemed to have died out, was revived (plates VI, 54 upper left quarter and 47, third large light from the left), possibly because the fiddle was growing larger, as plate 53 suggests, although it is notoriously difficult to scale instruments precisely from such iconographic evidence, or more probably because, with changing tastes in music, more agile and higher pitched instruments were required. The fiddle was essentially a tenor instrument, ideal for serious music by this time in which, as the name suggests, the tenor line was the most important, but less useful for light and rapid dance music, which was becoming more

popular, for which a treble instrument was far more suitable. This division, between the fiddles with their bias towards the lower pitches and the rebecs with their bias towards the higher pitches, was to last through the Renaissance, even after both instruments were made in complete families, as we shall see in the next chapter.

The other revival is that of the bowed rotta, an instrument which we last saw in plate 4. This can be seen at Westminster (plate 54, lower right quarter) and in the Beauchamp windows at Warwick some fifty years later (plate 55, second large light from the left). The Beauchamp instrument is so clearly drawn that we can see that the back of the neck is cut away, making it thinner than the sound box and more comfortable for the left hand. It was in exactly this form that the crwth survived into the last century in Wales. It is interesting to compare the bows of these instruments with those of the rebecs in the neighbouring window (plate 47). The bows of the crwthau have the 'hair' made of a laid rope in a single strand; presumably the bow hair should be tensioned by the player's thumb or a finger and not left slack as it is painted. One very often sees pictures of instruments held incorrectly or not properly tensioned, because neither the artist nor the model is a musician who knows how the instrument should be played; for this reason one has to be careful when reconstructing instruments or when trying to deduce playing styles from old pictures. The rebec bow is quite different: it is a blade of wood with teeth like a saw blade. Such bows are found today in several parts of Europe with folk instruments such as the Flemish bumbass which F. J. de Hen has described, and they may well have been used in this period also. One often sees, in illuminated manuscripts, jokes such as a pair of bellows bowed with a rake, but this is probably a serious and factual illustration.

Plate 45 includes a string instrument in the left-hand large light which makes its first appearance around this time. It may, like the clavichord, also be a derivative of the monochord, as has sometimes been suggested, but it may also be simply an extension of the rebec. It is here a long, narrow wooden box with a number of strings running along it, bowed and fingered as a normal string instrument. By the end of the century, it had changed radically and become what is usually called the tromba marina.

Plate 55 *Left to right:* bowl bell-chime, (censer), two harps, two crwthau, two lutes, two mandores. (*The Beauchamp Chapel, west half of the south window*)

Percussion Instruments

Other instruments which remained much the same include the percussion instruments. The nakers were more frequently snared than before (plates VI and 56); the timbre was still in use (plate 45, second large light from the left) as were the cymbals (plate 54, lower right quarter) and the triangle (plates VII and 58 extreme left) and many pictures show pellet bells attached to clothing. The tabor was more usually hung from the wrist than from the elbow or upper arm (plate VII) and different shapes were appearing (plate 47 left); the second large light from the left shows two players, one with the pipe and the other with the tabor. Both these tabors have a cloth fringe fitted to the rim of the drum, hanging down over the side of the shell. This fringe could be reversed and placed on the drum head to muffle the sound, as can be seen in plate 56, which is the first representation of muffled or muted drums that is known.

An instrument which was new at this time and which, while it appeared occasionally in the sixteenth and seventeenth centuries, did not become really popular until the late eighteenth century, is the musical bowls or resting bells shown at the top left of plate 55. We cannot tell the material of which they were made; they may be of metal or they may be of glass. This is the only angel instrumentalist who is playing from music in these windows. The angelic singers, whom we have not illustrated, are singing from music, music which is so accurately drawn, unlike the straight lines which only indicate music in plate 55, that C. F. Hardy was able to identify the hymn so that today it is performed each year in the Chapel.

Plate 56   The joust. Muffled nakers with snares and S-shaped trumpet. *c.* 1397. (*Misericord S 9, Worcester Cathedral*)

Wind Instruments

The Recorder

There was more change among the wind instruments than among the percussion. Small pipes, both two-handed pipes such as those in the third large light from the left of plate 45, and tabor pipes (plates VII and 47) continued much as before, but a longer duct flute came into use and one of these has survived (plate 57, left). This instrument was found beneath the ruins of a house in Dordrecht, Holland, and cannot be later than 1450 and may be anything up to a century earlier. It has seven finger holes, the lowest of which is duplicated so that it can be played by either the left or the right little finger, as the player prefers (the unwanted hole was plugged with wax) and it has a thumb hole. It is, in other words, what the French call a *flûte à neuf trous* and what we call in English a recorder and it is the earliest surviving example. It was originally straight and not curved; many much later instruments have also warped with time. Originally it had a beaked mouthpiece and a bell which fitted onto the tenons at each end and a reconstruction by Rainer Weber, on which these features are restored, can be seen beside it.

The Shawm

The shawms were beginning to grow into a family of instruments as can be seen on the extreme left of plate 45 and in the three right-hand large lights of plate 58, where three sizes are shown next to each other with the bass in the neighbouring window. The smallest was still the most common size (plate VII). There existed also a larger instrument with a bottle bell which may have been a bass shawm or may have been a straight trumpet; an example is in plate VI at the top left; the illustrations are never clear enough to determine which it is.

The Hornpipe

An instrument which survived into recent times in Wales as the pibcorn and in Scotland as the stockhorn and which is still used by the Basques as the alboka, is the hornpipe, several examples of which can be seen in plate 58 (left-hand large light and extreme right). This has a horn bell at the lower end to project the sound and a horn at the upper end also,

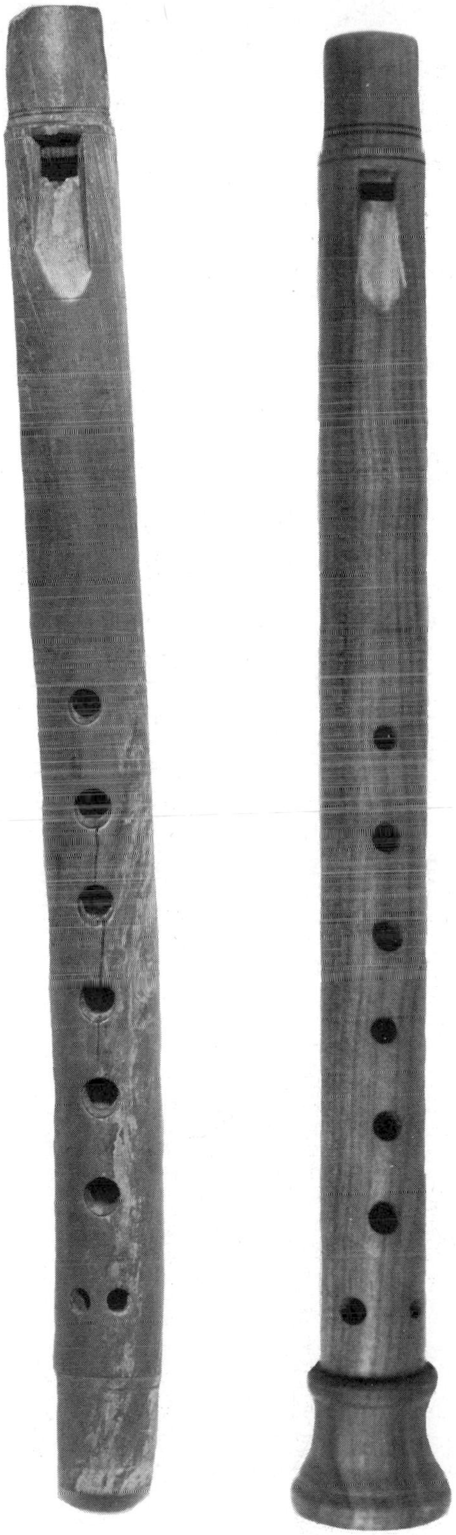

Plate 57 *Left:* Recorder found under a house in Dordrecht. *c.* 1390. (*Gemeente Museum, The Hague*); *right:* reconstruction of the same instrument with beak and bell by Rainer Weber, Bayerbach

Plate 58 *Left to right:* portative organ, triangle, single and double pibcorn, two alto shawms, two tenor shawms, two diskant shawms, double pibcorn. (*The Beauchamp Chapel, east half of the north window*)

The harmonic series

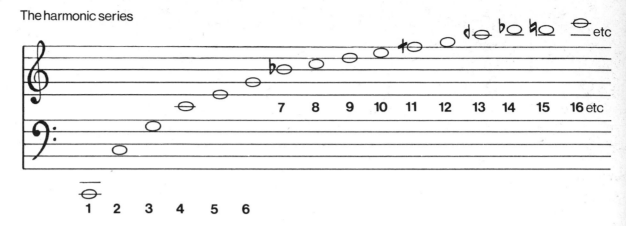

to serve as a wind-cap. Between the two horns is a pipe of reed, cane or wood in which the finger holes are bored. An idioglottal single reed of straw or cane, similar to that used in the drone pipes of many bagpipes today, is inserted into the upper end of the pipe and the horn wind-cap allows the player to blow the instrument without taking the reed into his mouth, which would otherwise wet it. The reeds therefore last much longer and do not alter their playing characteristics, as they would if they became saturated. Both single and double instruments are used in many areas and both single and double can be seen in the Beauchamp windows.

The Bagpipes

As in the earlier periods, both shawms and single reed pipes were blown through bags. Plate 45 extreme right shows a double shawm bagpipe, two conical chanters each with three or more finger holes, with one long cylindrical drone passing over the player's left shoulder. It seems to have been during the course of the fifteenth century that the various regional forms of the bagpipe became established, such as the Scots with a conical chanter and one or two short cylindrical drone pipes and the Flemish with the two very long cylindrical drones familiar from the paintings by Breughel and others. Whereas in the earlier Middle Ages much of Europe shared a common stock of instrumental resources, so that we see very similar instruments used over a wide area for all types of music, differentiation began in the fifteenth century; different instrumental sonorities are found to suit the peoples of different areas, and different types of instruments begin to be used for different styles of music.

Trumpets and Horns

While these differentiations were sometimes a matter of regional preference, they were also sometimes a matter of practical convenience or of acoustical necessity. The trumpet is a case in point. The old long trumpet was still used, but it was an inconvenient instrument to play; a length that was comfortable for players mounted on horse or camel back causes difficulties when played on foot, so that we see many illustrations similar to those in the Westminster Abbey Chapter House (plate 54, lower left quarter) which show a shorter instrument of similar type. However, convenient as these may have been for portability, their shortness limits their musical usefulness.

A trumpet without valves, slides, handstopping or finger holes can only produce the sounds of the harmonic series and the shorter the tube, the fewer the notes that can be played. The player is able to sound the harmonic he chooses by varying the tension of his lips, but there is a limit to how tight his lips will go and thus a ceiling above which only the most exceptional players can produce notes. As a result, the modern English hunting horn, some nine inches long, can only produce one note, the fundamental or first harmonic. Two are usually possible, and occasionally three, on a reasonably long cow or goat horn or oliphant (plate 7) and the notes in the gaps between these harmonics can be obtained by the use of finger holes or hand-stopping (plates 2 and 6). The modern bugler can produce the first half-dozen harmonics on his instrument, a tube about 4ft 6in long; the Westminster trumpets (plate 54) are about a foot shorter and were probably capable of at most the first four or five harmonics, depending

Plate VIII   Musician angels, Hans Memlinc. *Left to right:* psaltery, tromba marina, lute, folded trumpet, tenor shawm. *c.* 1480 (*Koninklijk Museum, Antwerp*)

Plate IX   Musician angels, Hans Memlinc. *Left to right:* straight slide trumpet, folded slide trumpet, portative organ, harp with brays, waisted fiddle with comb bridge. (*Koninklijk Museum, Antwerp*)

upon the skill of the players and upon the design of the mouth-piece and the shape of the bore. The narrower the bore in relation to its length and the sharper the bottom of the cup of the mouthpiece, the easier the higher notes become. The harmonic series forms a parabolic curve; the lower notes are far apart, gradually becoming closer together as the series ascends. A common chord is not complete until the 8th harmonic is achieved, and before one can play a scale one must be able to ascend to the 16th harmonic. The musical example above is schematic; it is conventional to write the harmonic series based on the low C, as it would sound on a trumpet about 8ft long. The actual pitches produced vary with the length of the instrument, but have the same interval relationship with each other. If an instrument of the trumpet family were to play a useful musical part, it was therefore as much a matter of acoustical necessity to have a long tube, to render the upper harmonics accessible, as it was a matter of comfort and convenience to have a short tube. Improvements in the technology of metal working allowed instrument makers to bend metal tubing without distorting it, and it is at this period that we first find instruments built either in continuous curves or in straight yards connected by U-bends (plates VI and 36). The folded trumpet became the standard European instrument for war and for ceremonial from this period onwards.

Sometimes it was folded in S-shape with a short middle yard, as in these plates, and sometimes it was more closely folded, in the overlapping shape that is more familiar to us today; at first with a short middle yard as in plates VIII and IX and later with all three yards the same length, as in plate 76. With such trumpets of either shape, it would be possible to play to at least the 8th harmonic and probably the 12th, which would have allowed the players of the fifteenth century, provided that they had trumpets of the correct lengths so that they were in the right key, to contribute a useful chordal part to any music and to play elaborate fanfares in military and ceremonial contexts.

An instrument which first appears in illustrations at this period is the jews harp. Archaeological evidence suggests that it was by no means new, for Roman examples have been found in a number of places. It is probable that either the Macedonians or the Romans brought it back from India. How it acquired its normal English name, nobody knows, for it is neither Jewish nor a harp. In several languages the word trumpet or trump forms a part of its name and there is some musical justification for this, since, at least in the lower part of its range, it also sounds the notes of the harmonic series, the player producing them by altering the shape and volume of his mouth cavity. In this way, the jews harp can play natural trumpet music. Its ability to produce non-harmonic pitches in the upper part of the range has recently been elucidated by C. J. Adkins.

The Practice of Music

Whereas in the earlier periods described in the first and second chapters, music had, apart from a few royal or quasi-royal secular and ecclesiastical establishments, been a matter for individual minstrels wandering across Europe, sometimes singly, occasionally in small groups, in the latter part of the fourteenth and the early fifteenth centuries, settled guilds of musicians became established in many of the towns of Europe. A town watchman was normally a musician, so that he might signal the hours from a convenient tower by day and, by sounding his instrument during his passage through the town, indicate that he was awake and performing his duties by night. He acted as a nucleus, attracting one or two other musicians who would join him to form a town band, the waits in England, the Stadtpfeiffer in Germany, to play on ceremonial occasions and to provide music for high days and holy days. Once such a band became established, the musicians became jealous of their rights; other musicians who came into the town would attract attention and, more important, would earn money that rightly belonged to the town musicians. And so the guilds began to be formed, groups of musicians who established that they, and only they, had the right to play for certain, or sometimes for any, occasions. Such guilds naturally limited their membership to the number that the amount of work in the town could support and they made it very difficult for any newcomers to gain admittance. At the same time, they acted as a benevolent society towards their own membership, taking some care of their retired members and their widows and orphans. The normal way of admittance

was by apprenticeship and the number of apprentices was normally strictly controlled and was sometimes limited to members' own children. A guild member was expected to be proficient on more than one instrument, so that a small group of players could provide a band of loud instruments for a street procession or a banquet, a band of soft instruments for an evening of music after supper, a dance band or a chamber group with equal facility. It might be the responsibility of the town council or the local land owner to provide the ceremonial instruments for official occasions, but the other instruments were usually the responsibility of the musicians themselves. This led to the establishment of instrument-making concerns in the larger centres and, in due course, to guilds of instrument makers as well as of instrument players. Just as the players needed mutual protection against outside competition, so did the makers. In addition, joint action was as necessary for them to protect themselves against unfair taxation and other encumbrances as it was for butchers, weavers or grocers.

The individual professional musician still existed, playing his way from court to court, from great house to great house and from tavern to tavern, but he had to be more careful than before of encroaching on the prerogatives of the town bands. In many places he might be safer in attaching himself to a troupe of performers who could put on an evening's entertainment than he would be travelling by himself.

The amateur musician continued to exist and his importance to the historian of music and musical instruments is great, for it was for such musicians, especially the wealthy, that many composers wrote and it was also for such musicians that instrument makers produced the more ornate and costly instruments that later generations thought worth the trouble of preserving. The ordinary amateur might lose or throw away his instruments, leaving them or their fragments to be found very occasionally by later archaeologists; the wealthy amateur had instruments of finely carved ivory (plate 7) or beautifully decorated wood (plates XIV and 19), some of which are now treasured in museums; the professional had plain and undecorated instruments which he used until they fell apart with wear and age and so are lost to us. Regrettably for our knowledge of the sonorities of early music, the more highly decorated an instrument, or the more costly the materials from which it is made, very often the worse its sound; to take examples from the later times more familiar to us, few professional musicians would play an ivory flute and none would tolerate the tone quality of an ivory lute, and yet many of both survive simply because ivory is obviously valuable and looks beautiful. As Eric Halfpenny once said: with rare exceptions only the bad instruments survive; the good ones are used until they reach the point of collapse; to which one might add that, in the case of string and keyboard instruments they are rebuilt and reconstructed to the extent that their original makers would hardly recognise them.

Nevertheless, our gratitude to the wealthy amateur is great, for even an over-decorated instrument gives us an indication of the forms used, besides remaining an object of beauty in itself. In addition, it was often the wealthy amateur, as well as the town council, who maintained a band of musicians and it was the fact that musicians were grouped into bands that created the demand for homogeneous groups of instruments, the consorts that were the ancestors of our orchestra. The beginnings of such a consort can be seen in the Beauchamp windows where, although the musicians are shown two by two, as they were in the *Cantigas* nearly two centuries earlier, in one case the pairs are grouped to show us, in plate 58 and on the extreme left of plate 45, a consort of shawms, an angelic wait-band, with two descants, two trebles, two tenors and a bass. The grouping of instruments into such consorts, like with like in the majority of cases, is one of the most important musical facts of the ensuing period of the Renaissance.

Chapter 4
The Renaissance

The Age of Maximilian—
The Flowering of the Renaissance, 1450–1600

While the professional musician flourished as never before in great establishments across Europe, the Renaissance is also the great period of the amateur. It was the period of the complete man, when a man of culture was expected to be a master of all culture; not merely to be a poet or a painter or a musician but to be all three. It was Italy, the land of Michelangelo and Cellini, to name only two such men, from which the Renaissance spread, impelled by the invention of printing, which enabled the new learning to travel at far greater speed and with far greater uniformity than had ever been possible before. As the Medici had in Florence in the previous century, the rulers of Europe vied with one another to become the greatest patrons of the arts, to attract the finest musicians, painters and sculptors to their courts. The most important of these for the historian of musical instruments was the German Emperor, Maximilian I, Maximilian the Great. Among the works of art executed for him was one that was left unfinished at his death in 1519, although planned nearly a decade earlier, his *Triumph*. This was to consist of a magnificent procession to illustrate his achievements and his pleasures and it is to our pleasure that music played a great part in this procession. One of the first groups is the fifes and the drums, the transverse flutes and the side drums (plate 59). Both were comparatively new instruments, introduced by the Swiss mercenaries who fought in all the armies of Europe; for another two centuries the transverse flute (plate 70) was called the Swiss pipe, until the favour of another monarch, Frederick

Plate 59   Side drums; by Hans Burgkmair. *c.* 1520. (The Triumph of Maximilian the Great)

the Great, won it the name of German flute. Next in the procession, after the bears and the butler, the chief cook and the tailor, comes a small consort of two viols and three lutes, the viols, another new instrument, both being tenors and the lutes treble, tenor, the mean or normal lute, and bass. Immediately after them we see (plate 60) a mixed group of wind instruments: one plays a basset shawm, the second a tenor crumhorn, the third has his back to us but appears to be playing another crumhorn, the fourth plays a tenor shawm and the fifth, who is identified as the master trombonist Neyschl, plays a tenor sackbut.

This group raises a problem since, as we know the instruments today, shawms and crumhorns are not compatible as an ensemble; either the crumhorn was a much louder instrument than it became later or, and more probably, we have here pictures of the never-precisely-identified dulcina or douçaine, the quiet shawm to which Tinctoris and other writers refer but of which there are no surviving specimens and no identified representations or precise descriptions. Immediately behind this carriage comes (plate 61) the court organist, Paul Hofhaimer, playing a positive organ with, behind his back, a regals shut in its case. After him comes a mixed band (plate 62), mostly of loud or dance band musicians: pipe and tabor, two rauschpfeife or wind-cap shawms and one of the newly invented violins, with two lutes, quintern or treble and bass, bass viol and harp. The next carriage bears the court Kapellmeister, Jorg Slakany, with choir and cornett and sackbut, and after them come

Plate 60   Alto and bass crumhorns, tenor and bassett shawms, tenor sackbut; by Hans Burgkmair. (The Triumph of Maximilian the Great)

the jesters, including players of the tabor pipe and jews harp. The next musical groups come further along the procession, when we see the Burgundian state pipers (plate 63): five rauschpfeif players, ten shawm players and ten sackbuts. Then, after representations of the Emperor's marriage with Mary of Burgundy (through whom he inherited the Burgundian territories), of his wars and his coronations, come the Imperial state trumpeters (plate 64), five kettledrummers and twenty-five trumpeters, of whom we show only a few. They, as is their right, precede the Emperor himself.

These woodcuts by artists such as Hans Burgkmair and Albrecht Dürer were executed in the last seven years of the Emperor's reign, between 1512 and 1519, and they show us how radically the range of musical instruments had altered in less than a century. This period, between 1450 and 1500, is one of the great watersheds; a man who lived in this time would, in his childhood, have heard the sounds of medieval instruments and in his old age the sounds of the Renaissance, just as a man living from 1625 to 1675 would have heard first the sounds of the Renaissance and later those of the Baroque, and as in the mid-eighteenth century a man such as Johann Christian Bach, a son of J. S. Bach and a teacher of Mozart, heard as a youth the Baroque orchestra and as an old man the Classical orchestra that became our

Plate 61 Paul Hofhaimer playing positive organ with regals encased behind him; unsigned. (The Triumph of Maximilian the Great)

86

own. It is our good fortune that the first of these epochs which saw, or rather heard, the entire sound of instrumental music change, coincided with the development of printing and with the thirst for knowledge at all levels of the community rather than just among the upper classes.

To this thirst we owe Sebastian Virdung's *Musica Getutscht*, published in Basel in 1511 with woodcuts by Urs Graf, which was the first of a long stream of books describing the musical instruments then in use and illustrating them. The woodcuts are often crude and sometimes inaccurate or uninformative, but for many instruments Virdung is the prime source and occasionally, with his

Plate 63   The Burgundian pipers: tenor shawms and tenor sackbuts; unsigned. (The Triumph of Maximilian the Great)

Plate 62   Broken consort: pipe and tabor, treble and tenor rauschpfeife, mean lute and quintern, violin or fiddle, harp with brays, bass viol; by Hans Burgkmair. (The Triumph of Maximilian the Great)

Plate 64 The Imperial
Trumpeters: timpani and
trumpets; unsigned. (The
Triumph of Maximilian the
Great)

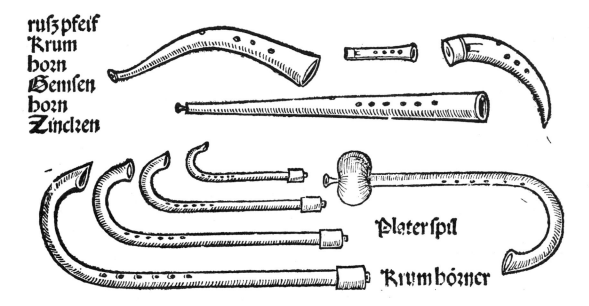

rußpfeif
Krum
horn
Gemſen
horn
Zincken

Plater ſpil

Krumhörner

Die ander art des zweite geſchlechts iſt in den holē roten die nit gelöcht ſynde
die doch ein menſch erplaſen mag welche aber von den ſelbē zū regulierē ſynd vñ
wie man dar uff lernen werd mögen dar von will ich hie nit mer ſage aber indē
andern büch will ich etwas nüws vñ ongeizntē dar von ſagen vnd ſchtyben

Plate 65   *Top left to right:* horn with finger holes, flageolet or short duct flute, gemshorn. *Centre:* cornett. *Below:* crumhorns, bladder pipe. 1511. (*Virdung* Musica Getutscht)

follower, Martin Agricola, who used Graf's illustrations with a few new ones of his own in his *Musica instrumentalis Deudsch* of 1528, the only source. The gemshorn (plate 65), a very popular instrument today in the revival of early music because of its easy technique and sweet tone, is known only in Virdung's and Agricola's illustrations. This same plate is also the evidence, the sole evidence, that finger-hole horns were still in normal use in the early sixteenth century. The Krum Horn of this illustration, literally crumpled horn, must not be confused with the Krumhörner, the hooked-ended, reed-blown instruments which Virdung illustrates on the same page of his book. Virdung was sufficiently interested in the whole art of music to illustrate folk instruments (plate 66), something in which his followers were less interested. Virdung shows the pot and spoon of the rough music, pellet bells of the type that we still use, a helically coiled horn, a huntsman's

instrument and the ancestor of the French horn of later generations, a watchman's horn, a cow bell, a jews harp and a combined pellet bell and clapper.

Virdung illustrates also the hurdy-gurdy, under the name of lyra. The body of the instrument has taken a more curved shape than those which we have already encountered and is now guitar-like in outline. A rather more ornate instrument of later sixteenth-century date survives in Paris (plate 67). Agricola copies Graf's woodcut and adds another showing a similar instrument which is played with a separate bow, instead of a wheel, and Praetorius, almost a century later, completes the set mentioned in the second chapter by illustrating a wheel-played instrument with a fiddle-type finger board. The hurdy-gurdy was still normally a folk instrument, often played by blind beggars who would find the wheel easier to manage than a bow and the key-operated tangents more certain than a normal finger

dañdas/welches einer ein harpfen hatgenennet/das heißt der ander eyn leyr/vñ
herwiderumb/vnd der gleichen vil/ Jch glaub auch/das in hundert iarn nechſt
vergangen alle inſtrumenta/ſo ſubtil/ſo ſchön/ſo gůt/vnd ſo wol geſtalt gema=
cht ſeind worden Als ſey Orpheus/noch Linus/noch Pan/noch Apollo/ Noch
keiner der poeten/hab geſehen oder gehöret/ vnnd das mer iſt müglich geachtet
hab zůmachen oder zů erdencken / Man findet auch ſunſt noch vil mer dorlicher
inſtrumenta=Die man auch für Muſicalia achtet oder heltet Als da ſtett·
Trumpeln/Schellē/Jeger horn/Acher horn/küſchellen·Brutſchē/vff dem hafen

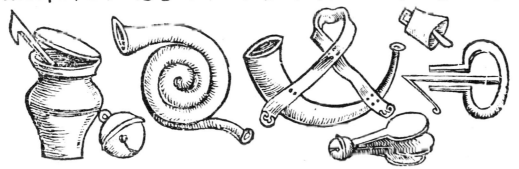

Auch ander mere/als pfeifflin auß den federkilen/lockpfeifflin der fogler / wach=
telbeinlin/Lerchen pfeifflin/Maiſen beinlin/ Pfeiffen von ſtrohelmen gemacht
Pfeiffen von den ſafftigen rinden der böm/von den pletern der böm/das mã ge=

board. A few highly-decorated instruments suggest
that the hurdy-gurdy was already attracting the
amateur, but in the main it remained a folk instrument.

Virdung illustrates also all the most important of
the instruments used for serious music making,
including a number of keyboards, among them the
clavicytherium. This is the upright harpsichord
which some scholars have suggested is the earliest
form of the harpsichord. The evidence of the
Beauchamp windows (plate 45) and of Arnault de
Zwolle's treatise (plate 48) seems to favour the wing
shape, which Virdung does not show, as the earlier.
He illustrates, with the harp and psaltery, the
dulcimer or Hackbrett, the hammered psaltery which
the Germans call a chopping-board, and among the
bowed strings, the gross Geigen, the big fiddles or
viols, the tromba marina or Trumscheit and the clein
Geigen, the little fiddles or rebecs (plate 68).

The tromba marina (plate 69) has changed since the
Beauchamp windows were painted (plate 45) and
resembles closely the instrument in Memling's panel
(plate VIII). The tromba marina is the only string
instrument which is played exclusively in natural
harmonics; the string is lightly touched with the
finger to compel it to break up into its aliquot parts.
The player touches it, for example, a quarter of the
way down its length to force it to vibrate in quarters
and produce the 4th harmonic; at a fifth of its length
for the 5th harmonic, and so on. In order to facilitate
this technique, the player bows above the stopping
finger, as can be seen in plate VIII, instead of fingering
on the upper part of the instrument and bowing on
the lower. It is presumably because it plays, like the
trumpet, exclusively in natural harmonics, that it is
called tromba; the origin of the marina part of the
name is lost in obscurity and controversy.

It is a characteristic of renaissance instruments that

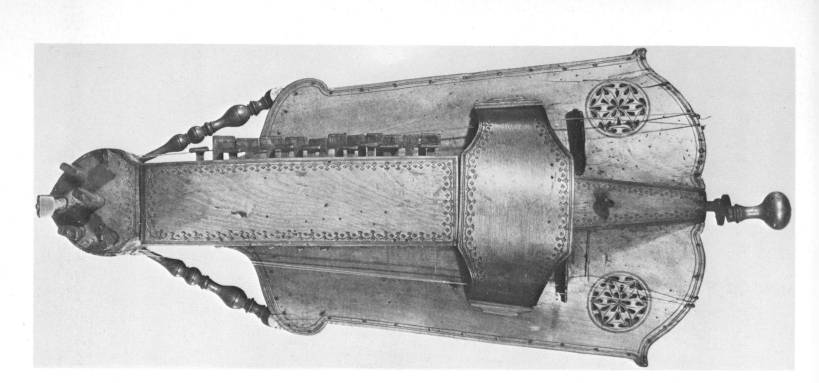

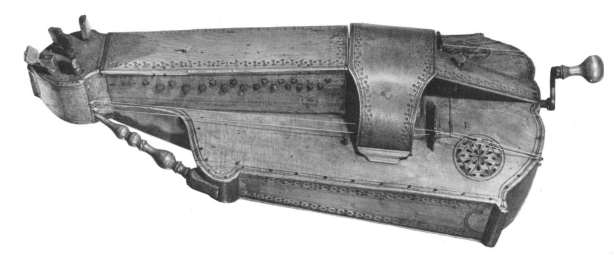

Plate 67   Vielle à roue or hurdy-gurdy. French 16th century. (*Conservatoire Museum, Paris E.2057*)

they were made in different sizes so that they could play together as families or consorts of like instruments. There were, for example, three principal sizes of rebec, the treble, the alto, the tenor and the bass. This apparent contradiction was true of many instruments. We find continual references to four sizes and illustrations to match with, very often, the two middle instruments identical in size. It would seem that, while the treble and the bass instruments were distinct, there was a tendency to play the inner parts on one instrument, using the upper or lower part of the range according to the voice required. Another example is Virdung's illustration of the recorders, one small, one large and two identical middle-sized instruments. On the other hand, the crumhorns are shown as four distinct sizes and this is probably because, whereas the recorder has a range of a couple of octaves, the crumhorn has a range of only just over one octave, thus necessitating two separate instruments to cover the middle parts.

Trumſcheit vnd clein Geigen

Des zweyten geſchlechts inſtrumenta der Muſica/iſt der lay/welche von dẽ hȯ len roren/vnd durch den windt geplaſen werdẽ/der ſind ich auch zweyerley art ſyn/Der roren ſynd etliche/welchen der menſch winds genůg mag geben/ oder die ein menſch erplaſen mag/Etliche aber mag kein menſch erplaſen/Zů vʒ ſelben můß man plaſpelge haben Der erſten art von den holẽ roṙẽ/die der menſch erplaſen mag ȯ ſynd ouch zweyerley/Etliche roren die haben lȯcher die tůt mᷓ mit den fingern vff vnd zů/vnd ſo vil ſye der lȯcher mer habẽ/ſo vil deſter beſſer vnd gewiſer mag man ſye reguliern/Doch hat ſelten eyn pfeiff über acht lȯcher Etlich ſynd aber nur von dryer lȯchern/Etlich von fiern/etlich vȯ fünffen/etlich von ſechſen/etlich von ſibnen/etliche von achten.

B iij

Plate 68 Rebec and tromba marina with bows. (*Virdung*)

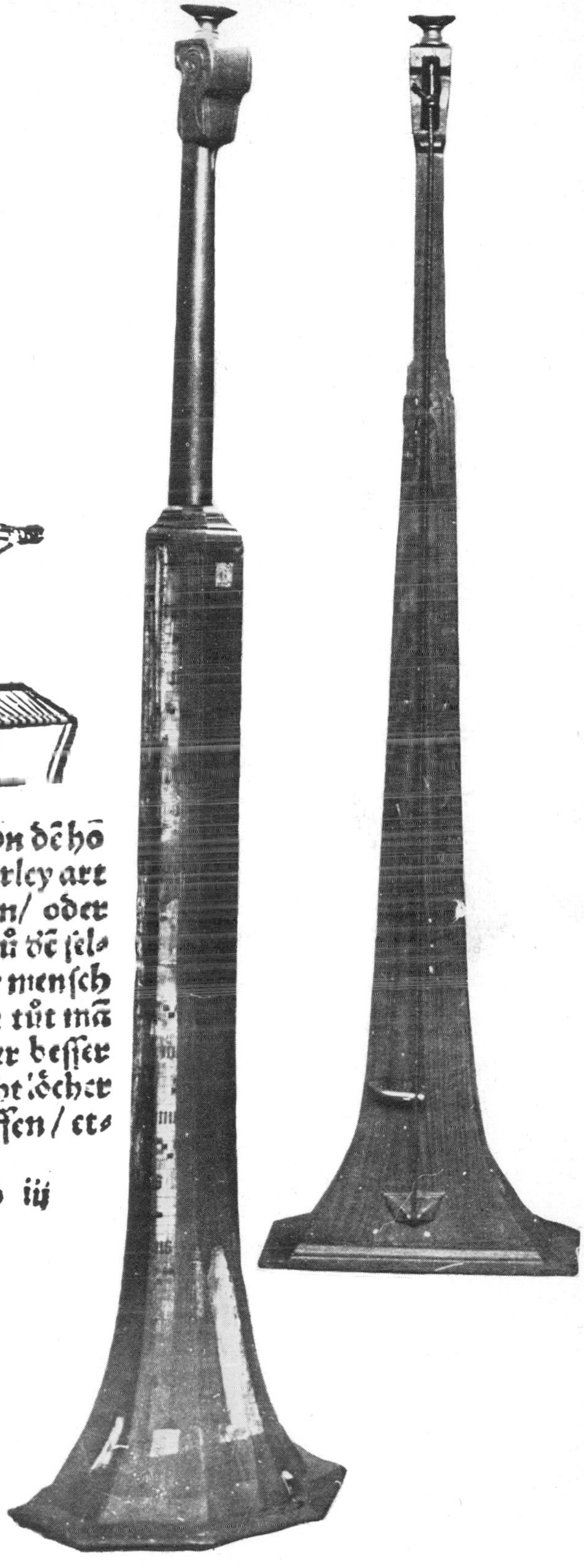

Plate 69 Trumscheit or tromba marina. German 16th century. (*Germanisches Nationalmuseum, Nürnberg MI 2*)

Plate 70   TRANSVERSE FLUTES
Right to left: descant, anon, 1062;
treble, anon, 1063; tenor, !! !!,
1065; bassett by C. Rafi, Lyons,
1066; bass in two pieces by
H. Vits, 2695. All 16th century.
(*Conservatoire Museum, Brussels*)

Opposite:
Plate X   Psalm 120 (to be
performed on the steps of the
Temple) *left to right:* pipe &
tabor, triangle, woodwind, long
trumpet, harp, two lutes, three
shawms, bagpipe, psaltery, tenor
shawm or cornett, portative
organ. King David watches from
a window. (The Isabella Breviary
[*f 184v.*] *British Library, Add
18851*) Flemish, *c.* 1490

Plate XI   'The Madonna of the
Orange Trees', Gaudenzio
Ferrari, 1529 or 1530. The first
painting to show a violin. (*The
altar-piece of San Cristoforo,
Vercelli*)

Plate XII   'Vanitas', Pieter
Claesz, 1597. Bass crumhorn with
two keys and sliders, violin, lute,
recorder. (*Rijksmuseum,
Amsterdam, 692–A2*)

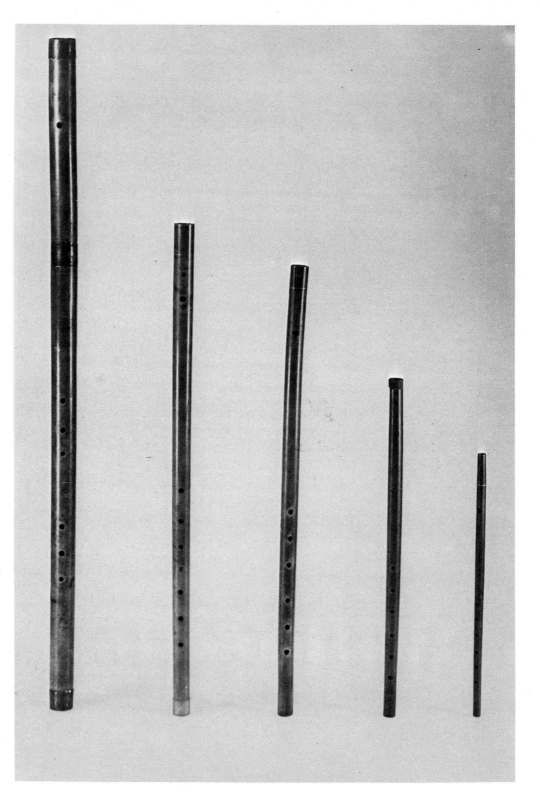

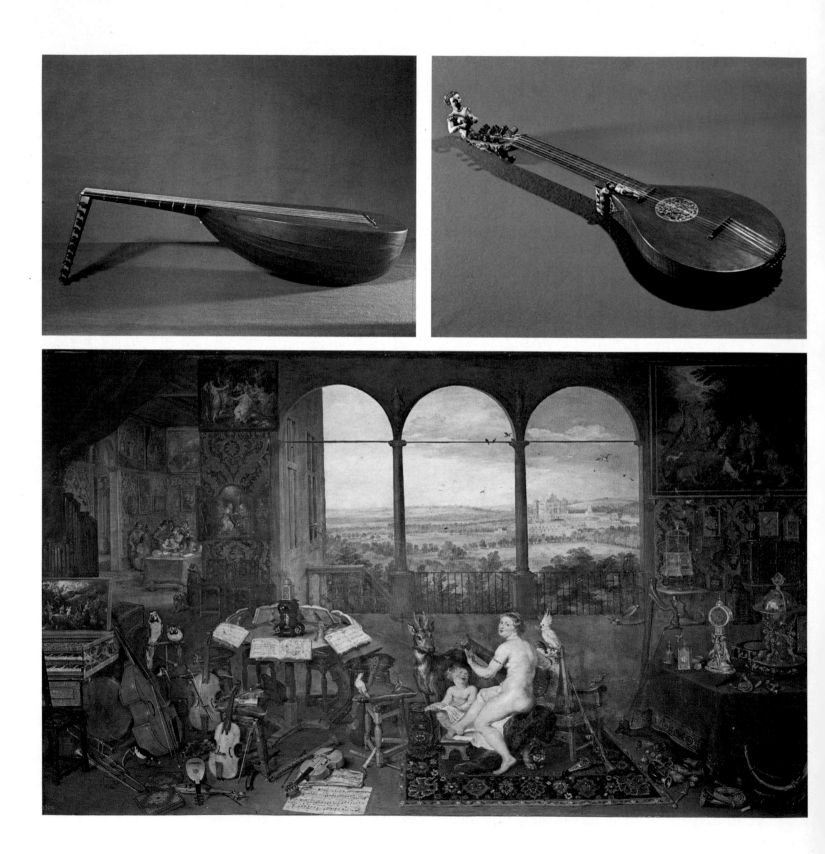

Woodwind Instruments

The Flute

From the fifteenth to the mid-eighteenth century, the recorder was regarded as *the* flute and, throughout this period, any references to flute without adjectival qualification always mean recorder; the side-blown instrument was called, in the sixteenth century, the Swiss pipe or fife or cross flute. Both flutes and cross flutes were made in different sizes. Plate 70 shows five sizes of cross flute, descant, treble, tenor (our modern orchestral flute), basset and bass, all of which are made from one piece of wood save for the bass, which is jointed between the embouchure and the finger holes. These instruments are the equivalent of our band flutes, from the fife down to the bass. Recorders were used in larger numbers, and often came in sets, all stored in one case. Such cases, one of which held fifteen recorders, figure prominently in the inventory of musical instruments drawn up for Henry VIII, and several survive in the Vienna collection. It is always difficult to assign renaissance recorders to specific voice names, alto, tenor, bass and so on, because, since they were made in one piece, they could not be tuned. In a time when different pitch standards prevailed, the only way to make instruments available for each pitch was to have a lot of instruments, all slightly different in size and hence different in pitch. The instruments in the Vienna collection are therefore grouped as follows, using the Praetorius group names:

I: Kleindiskant or Exilent, in high F (our sopranino), E flat, D, C and B (a semitone below our descant or soprano).

II: Diskant, in G or F (English treble, American alto), the right-hand instrument on plate 71, which is in G.

III: Alt, from E to C (our tenor); the next on the plate, which is in C.

IV: Tenor, from B down to G, all with a key to extend the reach of the lower little finger.

V: Bassett, from G to F (our bass); the next on the plate, in G.

VI: Bass, from D to B (our contrabass); the left-hand instrument on the plate, which is in C.

VII: Grossbass, from A down to the bottom C.

A unique example of a double great bass survives in Antwerp and is nearly twice the size of the largest shown here. It will be noticed that the names used in

Plate 71   RECORDERS
Right to left: diskant in G, G.S., C 145; alto in C, !!, C 160; bassett in G, !! ¡¡ !! and !! !!, C 175; bass in C, HIE.S, C 177. 16th century. None of the marks have been identified with a maker or even with a country. (*Kunsthistorisches Museum, Vienna*)

Opposite:
Plate XIII   Lute by Laux Maler, Bologna, *c.* 1520. The neck and peg box are late 16th or early 17th century. (*Kunsthistorisches Museum, Vienna, C 32*)

Plate XIV   Cittern made for Archduke Ferdinand of the Tyrol by Girolamo de Virchis, Brescia, 1574. (*Schloss Ambras collection. Kunsthistorisches Museum, Vienna, A 61*)

Plate XV   'The Allegory of Hearing', Jan Breughel, early 17th century. *Left to right:* double manual harpsichord probably by Hans Ruckers, positive organ, sackbut with two crooks, large side drum, violone, rebec, treble lute or quintern, bass viol, set of transverse flutes in a case, tenor viol, violin, cornett, shawm, lira da braccio, hand-bell, tenor viol, tenor cornett or cornone, tenor viol, recorder, straight cornett, lute, bell, harp, bells and pellet bells, half-moon and coiled hunting horns, French horn, sundry whistles and other noise makers. A music party in the background. (*The Prado, Madrid*)

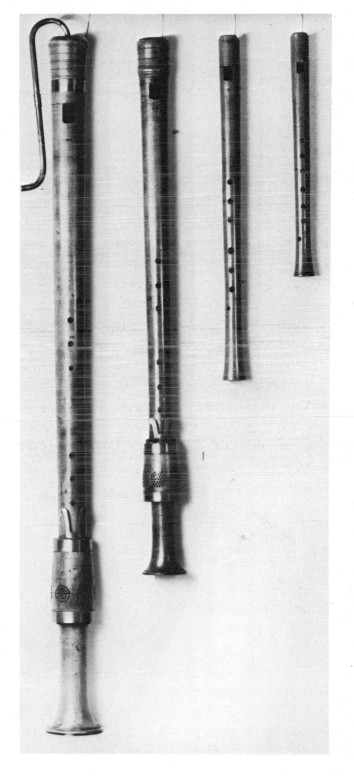

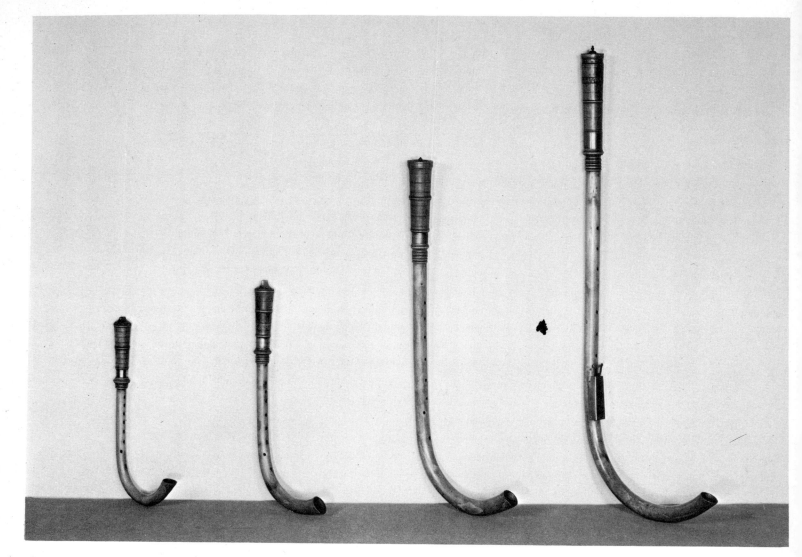

Plate 72 CRUMHORNS
Left to right: exilent, 673; diskant,
671; alt/tenor, 669; bass, 668.
Late 16th century.
(*Musikinstrumenten Museum,
Berlin*)

Vienna are one size different from those used today. There is considerable confusion over the correct terminology but it can be useful to follow the same guiding rule and to regard the smallest instrument with an extension key as the tenor and to scale the rest from that.

Early renaissance recorders were made with thick walls which enabled the maker to place the finger holes where they would be convenient to the hands. The finger hole is the orifice of a short tube through the wall of the instrument and its tuning can be controlled by the length, shape and diameter of this tube as well as by its position on the instrument; the thicker the wall, the longer the tube and the more control the maker has over its intonation. It will be seen that as the recorders grow in size, the two groups of finger holes get further and further apart. This was possible because, in a thick-walled tube, the finger holes can be drilled diagonally through the wood, the lowest hole in the upper group and the highest in the lower group having their inner openings much closer together than their outer orifices. This made for easier playing and allowed the makers to produce much larger instruments without the need for keys than the baroque and modern makers could do with their thin-walled instruments. Even those modern makers who are producing reproductions of renaissance recorders, with a few honourable exceptions, tend to economise on wood and to make instruments with thinner walls than the originals and they then find that they cannot place the finger holes as on the old instruments, so that either the player's comfort or the tuning has to suffer; only too often, both are bad.

The recorders do not appear in Maximilian's procession, probably because they were used for more intimate music-making than was suitable for such an occasion. They were the main wind instrument in Virdung's book and it is with the recorder that he teaches the techniques for all the woodwind. From this time onwards, it may well be authentic to use the recorder as the most prominent, the most common of the woodwinds. In the earlier periods, it was seldom seen in pictures, although we know from the Dordrecht instrument that it existed, and, as Anthony Baines pointed out in an address to the 1974 Conference of Musical Instrument Restorers in Nürnberg, the only excuse for using it as the leading instrument in medieval music-making is sheer laziness on the part of the players, who are happy with an instrument which is easy to play and cheap to buy. Much the same is true of the crumhorn, which has gained a popularity wholly unknown in its own day. There are very few illustrations of the crumhorn in use, there are not many literary references to it, and it appears to be an instrument which was newly invented in the early sixteenth century, so that its use for earlier music is quite unjustified.

The Crumhorn

The crumhorn is a derivative of the bladder pipe, which Virdung also illustrates and which we saw in the *Cantigas* (plates 26 and especially 27). The double reed is enclosed in a wooden cap, instead of in a bladder, which protects it from knocks and from the moisture of the player's mouth. The bore is cylindrical and it is a characteristic of cylindrical reed-blown instruments that they sound an octave lower than would a flute of the same length and that they overblow a twelfth rather than an octave if they can be persuaded to overblow at all. Since the player has not a sufficient number of fingers to cover all the holes necessary to obtain a range of a twelfth, it is not possible to produce a cylindrically bored reed instrument with a full compass unless one adds

closed-standing keys to cover additional holes and so, in effect, increase the number of fingers, as was done on the clarinet in the mid-eighteenth century to overcome precisely the same problem. Such key-work had not been invented in the Renaissance; the only keys used were open-standing keys on the larger instruments which extended the reach, and not the number, of the fingers so as to cover holes beyond the reach of the hands. Such keys were fitted to the bass crumhorn (plate 72), which also sometimes had sliders that could be pre-set to control the lowest note on the instrument, as can be seen in plate XII. Because the crumhorn could not overblow, its range was limited to a ninth, one note over the octave, and this is why the two middle parts required two separate instruments.

The Shawms

The crumhorn has a double reed, not unlike our modern bassoon reed. The other major family of double reed instruments was that of the shawms, the smaller of which we have encountered throughout the Middle Ages. Just as the crumhorns, rebecs, recorders and other instruments were made in families, so the renaissance shawm was also made in consorts, though evidence for the complete family, as it appears on plate 73, is lacking until fairly late in the sixteenth century. This plate shows shawms from descant to great bass, Schalmei to grossbass Pommer, but as so often in this period, none can be precisely dated. Judging solely by their appearance, particularly that of the smaller instruments in the group which are more slender than are some known early sixteenth-century examples (plate VIII), these are all late sixteenth century, possibly early seventeenth.

The shawm is blown with the reed set into a pirouette, which helps to support the player's lips and which can be seen in plate 63 but which has not survived on any of the instruments in plate 73. On the smaller sizes, the pirouette was set directly into the top of the instrument but the larger shawms would have been uncomfortable to play in this way and so a bent crook, similar to that of the modern cor anglais, was provided. The crook was usually bent to an angle of about 45° so that the bell of the instrument projected forwards except on the great bass, which had a crook like that of a bassoon. The great bass in Poznan is probably the only one to

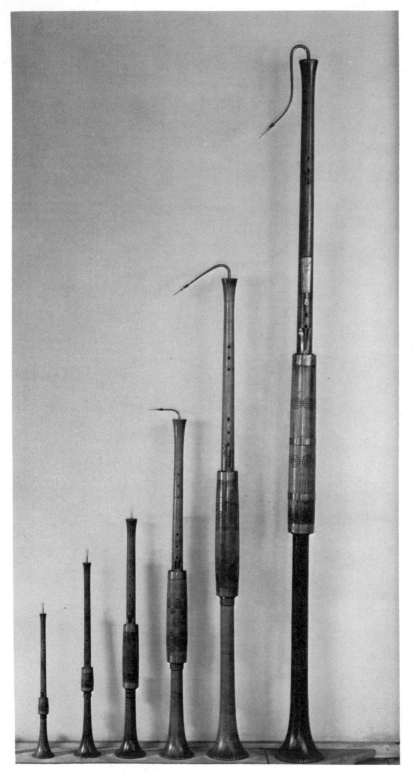

retain its original crook, which is 63.5cm long and allows the player to hold the instrument in the middle of its length with the bell well out behind him. As on the recorders, the key which extends the reach of the lower little finger is contained in a box called the fontanelle. Key construction was sufficiently crude that such protection was very necessary to avoid damage caused by casual knocks or by the key catching in the player's clothing. The fontanelle is pierced with small holes, normally in a decorative pattern, so that sound emitted through the key-covered hole should not be stifled. The larger instruments in plate 73 have more than one key, partly because the wood is thinner than on the shawm in plate VIII so that the maker has less latitude in the positioning of the holes and partly because, as the instrument grows, it is beyond the skill of even the most expert of makers to allow the fingers to cover the holes unaided; the great bass requires such a spread of the finger holes that keys are provided to extend the reach both up and down the bore.

The shawm has a conical bore and the tone is therefore loud and piercing, quite different from the firm buzz of the crumhorn. The difference is caused by the shape of the bore of the two instruments; the use of a wind-cap to cover the reed makes no difference in this respect, as is shown by the rausch-pfeif or wind-cap shawm. The only evidence for the existence of the rauschpfeif is Maximilian's procession (plate 62, the two instruments facing away from us), where the written description explicitly mentions a small and a large Rauschpfeif. On the basis of this description and illustration, Curt Sachs identified the three left-hand instruments on plate 74, which come from the Berlin collection of which he was curator, as Rauschpfeifen; if he was correct in this, as seems probable, the three right-hand instruments on the same plate, from the Prague collection where they are catalogued descriptively as wind-cap shawms, are Rauschpfeifen also. Experiment has shown that, when fitted with a suitable reed, these instruments produce an even louder sound than normal shawms;

the modern reproduction rauschpfeifen are not quite so loud, but this is a matter of the lack of accurate copies of historical instruments, something that bedevils the modern players of all early instruments. Rauschpfeifen must have been uncommon instruments, even in their own day, for very few of them survive and they appear neither in Virdung nor Agricola; Praetorius and Mersenne mention similar instruments, the Bassett or Nicolo and the hautbois de Poitou, but only fleetingly. It is presumably the fact that they are easier to play than normal shawms that has led to their frequent, and often anachronistic, use among medieval and renaissance ensembles today.

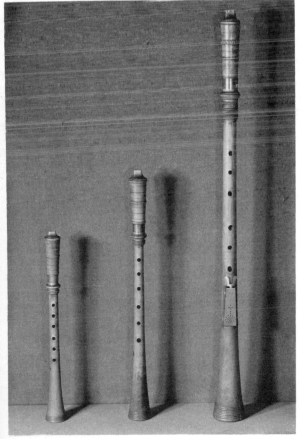

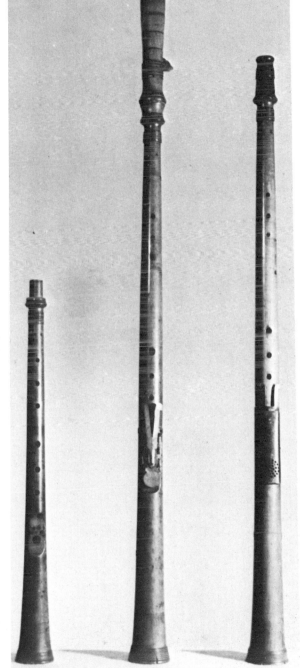

Plate 74 RAUSCHPFEIFE
Left to right: Descant, 74; treble, 665; alto, 667. (*Musikinstrumenten Museum, Berlin*). Tenor, 484E; bass, 486E; great bass, 487E. (*Národní Muzeum, Prague*). All 16th century

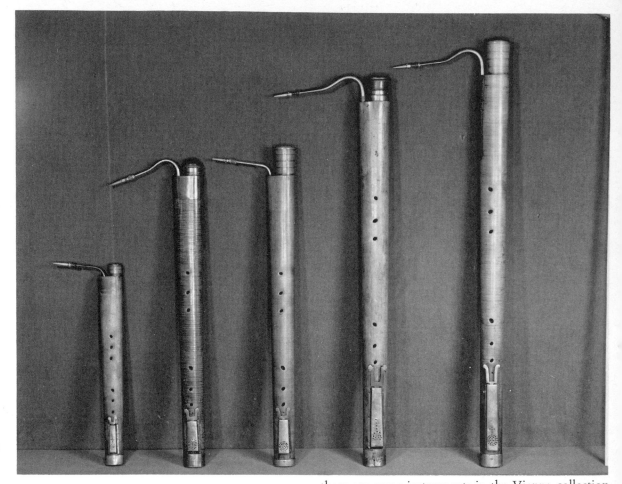

Plate 75   CURTALS AND DOUBLE CURTALS
Left to right: alt-Dulzian, 649; tenor-Dulzian, 652; gedäckt tenor-Dulzian, 650; gedäckt Choristfagott, 655; Choristfagott 654. (*Musikinstrumenten Museum, Berlin*)

The Curtal

It has been suggested that the curtal (plate 75) may have been invented simply because of the difficulty of holding the great bass shawm. Some authorities deny this, pointing out that the ratio of conicity to bore-length, and thus the tone of the instruments, is different and that the curtal is no more the bass shawm than the bassoon is the bass oboe. This is true enough and yet it may be that the curtal was invented for this reason and that the bore is narrower simply for lack of pieces of wood thick enough to make a true shawm bore in the shape of a curtal and because no players had large enough hands to hold such an instrument if it were made. The curtal consists of two conical bores drilled down one piece of wood, joined at the bottom by carving a linking horizontal bore and then plugging the lower end or butt with a cap. The curtal is the ancestor of the bassoon and there are some instruments in the Vienna collection with features both of curtal and of bassoon. As on the bassoon, the six finger holes are drilled into the narrower of the two bores, that from the reed to the butt of the instrument, and the thumb holes and keys are drilled into the wider part, that from the butt to the bell. Like all other renaissance instruments, the curtal was built in a family of sizes, from alto on the left of plate 75 to bass, on the right. There were two types of curtal, the one with an open bell and the other capped or *gedäckt* with a cap like the top of a pepper pot, which muted the sound. The name of the instrument in German depended upon its pitch. Just as the small shawm was *Schalmei* and the large, *Pommer*, so the small curtal was *Dulzian* and the large, the double curtal in English, *Choristfagott* and for even larger instruments, *Doppelfagott*. The lowest note of the double curtal was C, the same pitch as the bassoon without the bell joint.

Brass Instruments

The Trumpet

Virdung shows three distinct types of trumpet: a wide-bored instrument, the field trumpet or military instrument; a longer and narrower-bored instrument, the clareta, which was the musician's instrument, and the tower trumpet, used by the town band to play chorales and similar music at set hours during the day from the tower of the town hall or of the principal church. The two former instruments are folded in overlapping shape, like those of Maximilian (plate 64) and the instrument in plate 76, but the last, the tower trumpet, is still folded in the S-shape of the previous century (plates VI and 56). Since a natural trumpet can play only the notes of the harmonic series (p. 76), it may be wondered how it was possible to play chorale melodies. The technique is revealed by a number of pictures, though few are as clear as Memline's panels, particularly plate IX, which shows the trumpeters pressing the mouthpiece of the trumpet to their lips with one hand. The mouthpiece had a long stem, usually extending right down to the first bow or to the first boss of the straight trumpet. With the other hand, the trumpeter moved the whole trumpet away from the mouthpiece, thus sliding this stem in and out of the main tubing. Altering the length of the tubing alters the pitch of the whole series. If one starts with a tube some 8ft long, producing the series on C, lengthening the tube by about a foot lowers the pitch a tone and six inches by a semitone, so that it is possible to fill the gaps between the harmonics from the 3rd harmonic upwards and thus to play any normal chorale part.

The ordinary trumpet was used for military signals and other fanfares, for tuckets (Italian, *toccata*) and sennets (Italian, *sonata*) and, in German, *Aufzug* and *Auszug*, short processional flourishes, which, as technique improved, became more and more elaborate. Players learned to climb higher and higher in the harmonic series, developing the clarino technique of playing from the 12th harmonic upwards. It must be emphasised that clarino was a part of the trumpet range and, by extension, parts written in that range and players of those parts; it was never a special instrument. Clarino parts were played by specialist players on normal trumpets with no

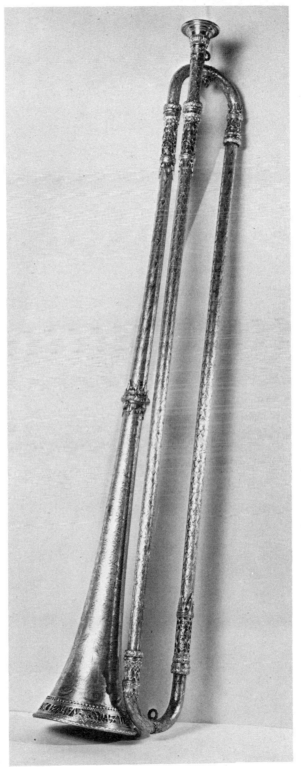

Plate 76 Trumpet with original mouthpiece, by Anton Schnitzer the elder. Nürnberg, 1581, Λ 258. (*Kunsthistorisches Museum, Vienna*)

artificial aids save for their own skill. With this skill, which included the ability to lip the out-of-tune harmonics such as the 11th and 13th into tune, the trumpet became by Monteverdi's time a fully melodic instrument, which it remained until the mid-eighteenth century when the technique died out.

In Germany, and to a lesser extent in other countries, the use of the trumpet was severely restricted to noblemen above a certain rank and to certain privileged cities and regiments. Trumpeters were formed into guilds and took very strong measures to prevent others from playing the instrument, going so far as to destroy the instruments and break the teeth of any who tried to encroach upon their rights. The result of these restrictions was two-fold: on the one hand, the players were able to elaborate their technique and to ensure that players were fully capable before being allowed to call themselves trumpeters, but on the other hand the musical use of the trumpet was circumscribed and restricted more than that of other instruments.

The Sackbut

The slide trumpet, or *tromba da tirarsi*, was efficient enough in slow-moving music such as chorales, but moving so much weight in and out was not practicable for faster melodies for, unless it were held very steadily, the mouthpiece would wobble against the lip and cause the player to crack a note. This difficulty was resolved by refolding the tower trumpet slightly and placing the slide in the front bow, an arrangement which had the additional advantage that, since two parallel sections of tubing were moving, half the forward movement extended the same total amount of tubing. The resulting instrument was called sackbut in English, *Busaun* and later *Posaun* in German and *trombone*, or great trumpet, in Italian. The sackbut was made in various sizes, of which the alto, tenor and bass were the most common and the tenor the most important. A number of tenor sackbuts can be seen in Maximilian's *Triumph* and it is an interesting side-light that the master-trombonist of the court, shown in plate 60, was the father of Jörg Neuschel, the maker, in 1557, of the second oldest surviving dated trombone, again a tenor, which was once in Canon Galpin's collection and which is illustrated on plate 42 of his *Old English Instruments of Music*. Other scenes from

the procession show (plate 63) the sackbut acting as the bass to a group of shawms, a function that it often retained even after the bass shawms and curtals came into use, and a sackbut and cornett accompanying a choir. The sackbut was the natural accompaniment for voices because, as well as being able to play loudly or softly at will, an ability shared only with the cornett, organ and drums among renaissance instruments, its slide enabled it to play absolutely in tune, something that was far more difficult to achieve with the finger holes of most other wind instruments. All finger holes are placed in compromise positions, as nearly as possible in the right place for the fundamental octave and for the overblown octave, but the two are seldom precisely the same, in addition to which the maker must keep the holes within the reach of the fingers. The sackbut has no such problems, for the slide positions are infinitely variable, and it retained this rôle of vocal accompaniment throughout the sixteenth, seventeenth, eighteenth and nineteenth centuries. In the music of the church it was normal to score the alto sackbut in unison with the alto voice, tenor with tenor and bass with bass; the descant was rarely used, the tone of the cornett or Zink being preferred. Tenor and bass sackbuts can be seen on plate 77. The left-hand tenor, by Erasmus Schnitzer and dated 1551, shows the older form of the bell; the right-hand tenor the late sixteenth-century form. The right-hand bass is, strictly, just beyond our period, being dated to 1612 but is of interest since it has an additional slide in the back-bow which is operated by the plunger projecting forwards from it; this allows the player to alter his tuning from choir pitch to chamber pitch. The handle attached to the lower stay on both basses is necessary because the extension of the slide is greater than the arm can manage unaided.

The Cornett

The upper voices of the choir were supported by the cornett (plate 78), which was the refined descendant of the finger-hole horn. The cornett was usually made of wood, though occasionally of ivory. There were two basic types: the ordinary curved instrument with a separate, cup-shaped mouthpiece like a miniature trumpet mouthpiece (the two left-hand instruments on the plate), and a straight instrument, the mute cornett, with an integral, conical mouth-

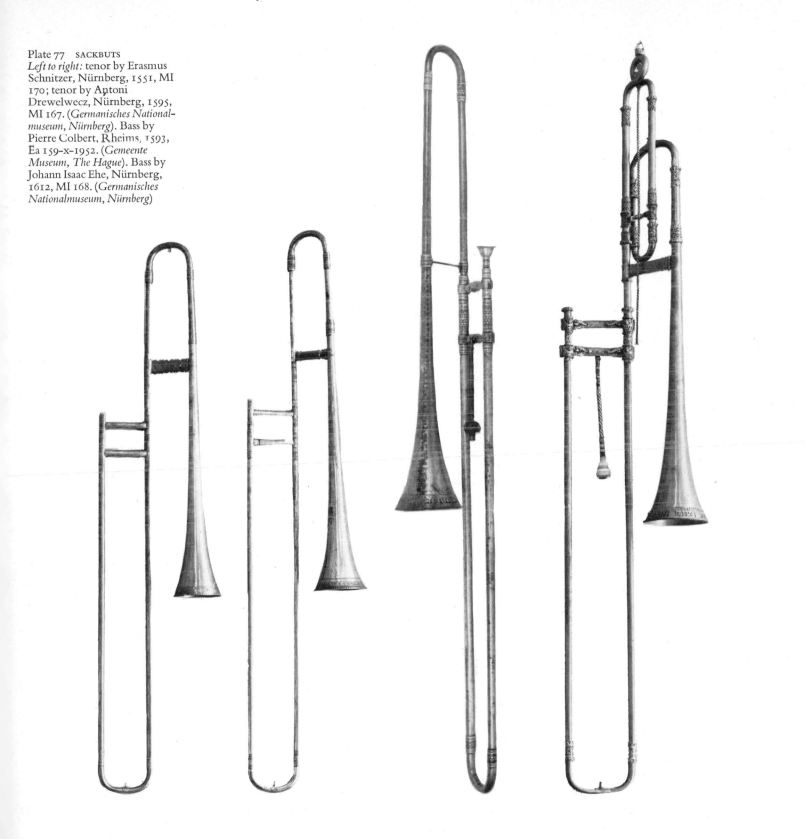

Plate 77   SACKBUTS
Left to right: tenor by Erasmus
Schnitzer, Nürnberg, 1551, MI
170; tenor by Antoni
Drewelwecz, Nürnberg, 1595,
MI 167. (*Germanisches National-
museum, Nürnberg*). Bass by
Pierre Colbert, Rheims, 1593,
Ea 159-x-1952. (*Gemeente
Museum, The Hague*). Bass by
Johann Isaac Ehe, Nürnberg,
1612, MI 168. (*Germanisches
Nationalmuseum, Nürnberg*)

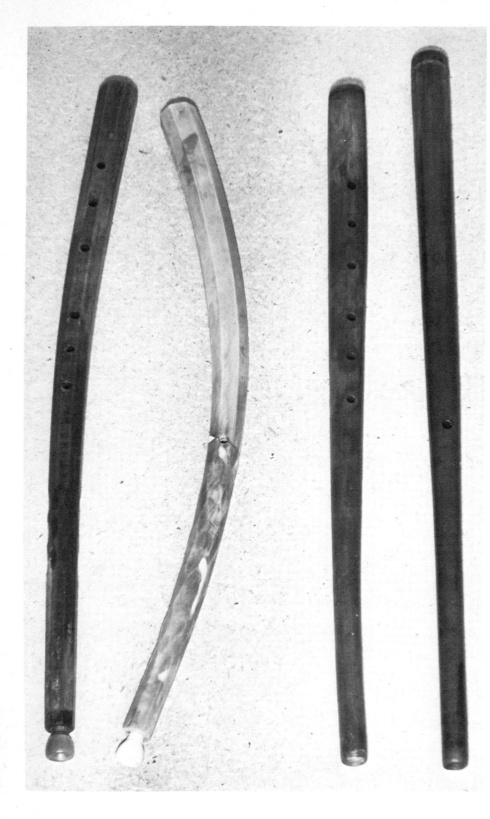

piece, like that of a horn, carved into the top of the tube (the right-hand instruments on plate 78), which was much quieter in sound. The straight cornetts were bored on the lathe but the curved ones were made by splitting a piece of wood, carving out the bore and reuniting it; they were often covered with leather to help to seal them against leakage. Various sizes were used, from the cornettino down to the contrabass. The smaller normal instruments were sometimes made straight, but can always be distinguished from the mute cornetts by the presence of the separate mouthpiece; the larger sizes were usually made in serpentine shape and examples of various sizes can be seen in plate XV. The bass cornett was rare and the contrabass very rare since their tone was not comparable to that of the serpent due to their narrow bore. R. Morley Pegge described one of the two surviving contrabass cornetts in some detail in his article on the anaconda.

The mute cornett was always quiet in sound but the curved instrument could be played loudly or softly at will. It was used for tower music, when it had to compete not only with the trumpets or the sackbuts but with the street noises below, but it was compared by Mersenne in the seventeenth century with a gleam of sunlight, which suggests a quiet sound, a suggestion which is confirmed by his statement that an expert player could sustain eighty or a hundred *mesures* in one breath; whether *mesures* means bars or beats, this is an incredibly long time.

It is a truism that the favourite instrument in any period is that which is most often compared to the human voice. In the sixteenth and seventeenth centuries, this was the cornett, which was the great virtuoso instrument of the Renaissance. The revival of early instruments has taught us just how difficult the cornett is to play even tolerably, let alone well, and makes us realise that, despite our feeling that nobody has ever played instruments as well as we do, the great virtuoso flourished in every age and need fear no comparison with modern players.

The serpent differs from the bass cornett only in that it is much wider in bore and therefore is more suited to bass parts. Its use in this period seems to have been confined to the church.

The Horn

As we have observed, the short horn was used at

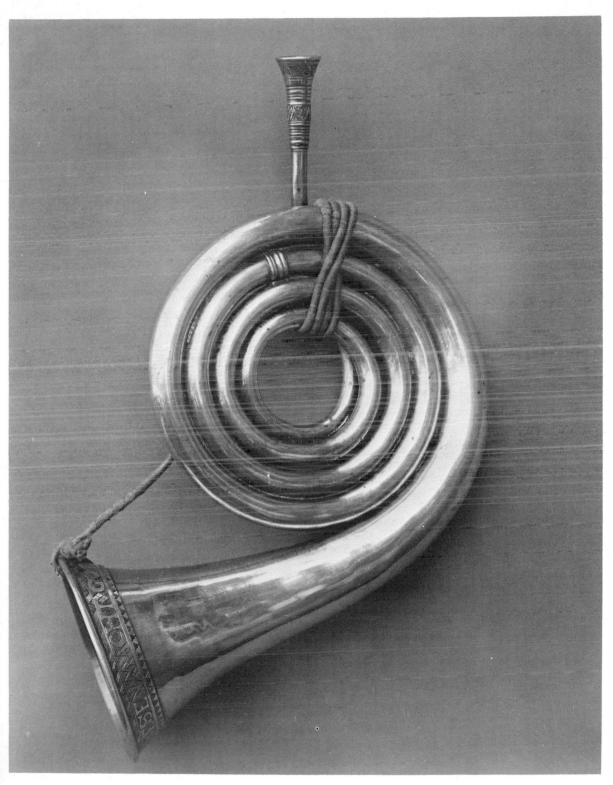

Opposite:
Plate 78   CORNETTS
Left to right: treble cornett
marked MS, 3065; rear view of
ivory treble cornett, 580; mute
cornett, 3066; rear view of mute
cornett, 661. All 16th or early
17th century. (*Musikinstrumenten
Museum, Berlin*)

Plate 79   Helical horn marked
Gott ist mein Helfer V.S. zu
Dresen macht. *c.* 1570.
(*Staatliches Historisches Museum,
Dresden*)

Plate 80 Pair of timpani,
German, early 17th century.
(*Private collection, Holland*)

all periods. As metal workers became more skilled during the sixteenth century, they learned the art of bending tubing of brass and silver, either in the shape of the conventional trumpet or in more ornate patterns to suit the whim of wealthy potentates. They learned also to coil tubing, at first clumsily (plate 66) and then with greater skill (plates 79 and XV, on the table at the right and on the floor at its foot). Plate 79 shows the earliest known French horn, as we would call it today, an instrument in the Dresden collection pitched in highest A flat in modern horn terms. The tubing is coiled helically and the mouthpiece, unlike that of most brass instruments, fits outside the tubing instead of inside. The horn on the floor in plate XV is larger and probably sounded in high D or even lower; there is another, rather later horn in Dresden (both are illustrated in Morley Pegge's book) which is in D.

The earliest known use of the horn in a musical performance is mid-seventeenth century, but it is axiomatic that useless artifacts are not produced. If horn playing in the sixteenth century consisted only of rhythmically repeated single notes, no maker would produce and no customer pay for instruments such as these. Hunting had patently become sufficiently elaborate a ceremony that horns capable of playing

hunting calls up to the 8th harmonic or above were required.

Percussion Instruments

Both Virdung and Maximilian's *Triumph* illustrate timpani and side drums (plates 59 and 64). The timpani were newly imported from the east, the result once again of war between Christians and Muslims. Not invasions of Muslim lands by Christians, such as had produced the nakers, but an attempt by the Turks to overrun eastern Europe after their conquest of Constantinople. The Turks carried their large kettledrums on camel-back; the Hungarians adopted the instruments and mounted them on horse-back and later in chariots. They spread to all the courts of Europe and became the great emblems of state and royalty, their use being restricted in the same way as that of the trumpet and their players being members of the trumpeters' guilds. The first pair in England were imported by Henry VIII, probably in emulation of Maximilian. The majority of illustrations show them, as in plate 64, swathed in banners so that few details can be seen, with the result that it is very difficult to date surviving pairs with any precision. The pair in plate

80 appear to be late sixteenth or early seventeenth century in date.

Little early timpani music has survived; the player was expected to concoct a bass part to fit what the trumpets were playing. Enough is known of contemporary practice to say that wherever trumpets are used in groups, timpani would also have been used, and that when a score calls for trumpets (for example Monteverdi in *Orfeo*), timpani are implicitly included. The timpani were the first drums to be tuned to definite pitches and the normal convention, until Beethoven introduced new concepts, was to tune one drum to the keynote of the music and the other to the dominant or fifth of the key, the equivalents of the trumpets' 3rd and 4th harmonics. This use of definite pitches demanded more accurate tensioning of the skins than could be achieved with the rope tensioning that had been used and so tuning by square-headed bolts which screwed into lugs fixed to the shell was adopted. These bolts, which can be seen in plates 64 and 80, were turned by a loose key which is illustrated by Praetorius on his plate XXIII.

Two well-known paintings indicate that there was enormous variation in the size of the early side drum: Dürer's shawm player and side drummer in Cologne shows a drum perhaps six inches in diameter and depth; Rembrandt's 'The Night Watch' in Amsterdam shows a drum over two feet in each dimension. Both sizes are illustrated by Virdung but only the larger is referred to in the best-known book on the subject, Thoinot Arbeau's *Orchésographie* of 1585, in which the military drum is described as thirty inches in diameter and thirty inches in depth, an instrument of massive proportions. Arbeau was the first to print side drum beatings, indicating that the drum was played incessantly on the march, for he gives the number of beatings to the league.

One percussion instrument which Virdung omitted, but which Agricola added in his version of the book, is the xylophone (plate 81). The wooden bars which produce the sound were laid on hanks of straw tied to wooden struts, hence the German name of *Strohfidel;* this method of construction lasted well into the nineteenth century and even into the twentieth. Agricola's xylophone has the same tuning as some early keyboards: diatonic with both B flat and B natural, German B and H. The German names for the notes are another indication that B flat was the

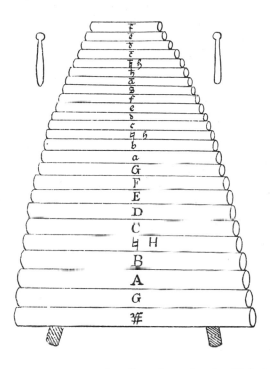

Plate 81   Xylophone and beaters. 1528. (*Agricola*, Musica Instrumentalis Deudsch)

commoner note in the diatonic scale, the H being either an adaptation of the natural sign or standing for *hoch*, the higher D. Many illustrations of a skeleton playing a xylophone, one being by Holbein, indicate that the xylophone was well-known in Europe in the sixteenth century and that the connexion between the rattle of the xylophone and the clatter of dry bones was common long before Saint-Saëns wrote his *Danse Macabre*.

Other percussion instruments such as cymbals and triangle and timbrel continued in use through this period, as did the pipe and tabor (plate X). François Merlin and Jacques Cellier, who produced an encyclopaedia for Henry III of France, illustrated many instruments, among them a group of drums (plate 82), distinguishing the French drum, the side drum, from the village drum, the pipe and tabor, and from the Basque drum, the timbrel or tambourine, which is shown with pellet bells on the frame instead of the more usual miniature cymbal jingles. The timpani are called German drums and, although this illustration is nearly seventy-five years later than Maximilian's, they are clearly shown as rope tensioned.

Their drawing of the triangle (plate 83), confusingly called Cymbale, shows the frame without

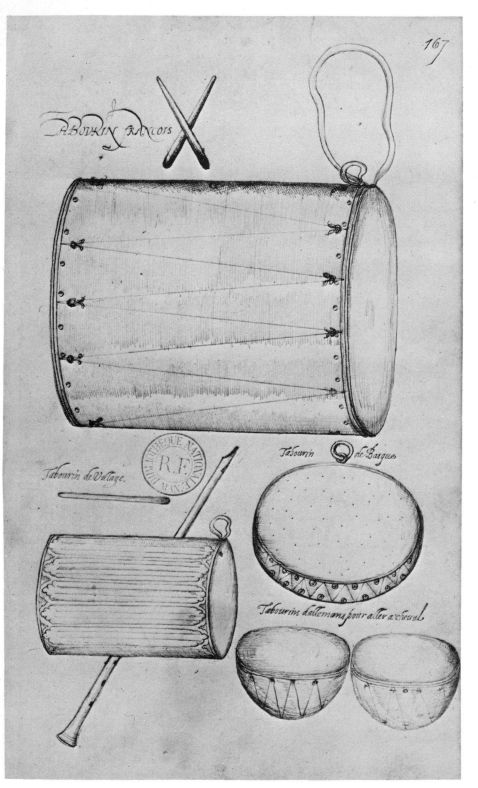

a gap and also the rings which produce the continuous susurration so different from the ting of the modern triangle. These rings appear in many other sources and remained a feature of the triangle until the beginning of the nineteenth century.

Merlin and Cellier illustrated also the carillon (plate 84), one of the earliest pictures to show the bells in their tower and the keyboard with the tracker wires linking the two. The accompanying text links the carillon firmly with the Low Countries, the area where its use is still centred today. Unlike the ordinary church bells, which are swung by a rope, the bells of the carillon are stationary and are struck by hammers. This technique permits a much more rapid action, so that tunes can be played on the bells. The carillon can either be played from a keyboard, as illustrated, or by a mechanical barrel on which tunes can be set. The barrel mechanism operates by clockwork and can be set in motion by a lever from a clock, so that the carillon could take the place of the tower musicians and provide music at certain hours through the day.

String Instruments

Just as in the earlier periods, and just as in the later Baroque, Classical and Romantic periods, the most important instruments for serious music making were the strings. Although the wind and percussion were used in serious music, as well as in processional and dance music, it was the lute, the consort of viols and, by the end of our period, the family of violins for which the best music was written. And this is said deliberately; we are reaching the period in which music was conceived for certain sonorities. Much music was still casually conceived: composers would write occasional music for the instruments which were to be available on that occasion and much of the dance music, in particular, was written for four or five parts, to be played on whatever instruments happened to turn up, but by the middle of the sixteenth century we find music written for fixed combinations and, by the end of the century, we have music that it would be unthinkable to play on any instruments but those for which it was envisaged. One example is Thomas Morley's *First Booke of Consort Lessons*, published for the Treble Lute, the Pandora, the Cittern, the Base-Violl, the

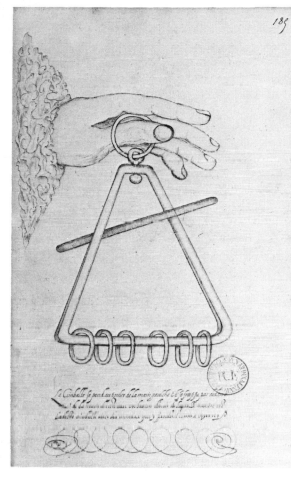

Plate 83   Triangle with six rings.
(*Merlin & Cellier* [*f 185*])

Plate 84   (*Right*) Carillon with
keyboard with eight keys and
eight trackers leading to nine
bells. (*Merlin & Cellier* [*f 188*])

Plate 82   (*Left*) Drums: *top to
bottom:* side drum, timbrel, pipe
and tabor, timpani. 1585. (*Merlin
& Cellier*, Recherche de plusieurs
Singularités [*f 167*.] *Bibliothèque
Nationale, Paris, français 9152*)

Flute and Treble-Violl (though, as Thurston Dart pointed out in his review of Sydney Beck's edition of the work, the music is clearly written for the violin and the treble viol is only specified in the hope of it selling better for that instrument). Another is John Dowland's *Lachrimae* or *Seaven Teares figured in Seaven Passionate Pauans* for the Lute, Viols or Violons, but which is very obviously written for the viols.

The Viols

The viols grew out of the medieval fiddle and seem to have appeared quite suddenly. The fiddle was illustrated as quite a large instrument, at least the size of the modern viola and sometimes larger, but it was nevertheless always played upwards, either on the shoulder or across the chest. Now, in the early sixteenth century, we suddenly have a family of instruments, all of which are played downwards, held either on or between the knees, according to size, but still called fiddle, in Germany at least. Virdung and Agricola call them *gross Geigen*, large fiddles, to distinguish them from the *clein Geigen*, the rebecs and, by Agricola's time, the violins which were just beginning to appear. In Italy they were *viole* (*viola* in the singular), as the fiddle had been in Latin (plate II) and *viole da gamba*, leg fiddles, to distinguish them from the *viole da braccio*, arm fiddles or violins which were later named more definitely from the smallest, and commonest, member of the family, the little viola or violino.

The early sources all show the same shape, with a deep waist and sharp upper and lower bouts (plate 62, extreme left). There are two early viols of this shape in Oxford, in the Ashmolean Museum, but the majority of the surviving early instruments are quite different in appearance. Plate 85 shows a range of viols, fairly typical in shape for their respective periods. The two left-hand instruments are part of a consort from about 1550; the right-hand viol dates from 1585 and the smaller viol between these was also made *c.* 1550. The body had become much slimmer than it was in plate 62, although by 1550 it is beginning to fill out again, and in particular the narrow shoulders seem to be a characteristic of the sixteenth century viol from the middle of the century. Not until the early seventeenth century do the shoulders fill out again into the shape that became normal for the baroque viola da gamba (plate XV). By the middle of the sixteenth century, six strings had become the usual number, although, as at the beginning of the century, five or seven are sometimes encountered.

Ian Harwood has pointed out that the sixteenth century viols had no sound post and no bass bar. The result was that a consort of viols had a wiry intensity in the Renaissance, quite different from the plummier sound of the baroque viols. Both sound post and bass bar seem to have been fitted to the viols in an attempt to increase their volume when they were already competing with the violins. The early viol, like the lute, depended chiefly upon the vibration of the belly for its sonority; the main function of the sides and back was to contain the resonating body of air and to act as a reflector of the sound waves. The bridge was lower than it was to become in the following century and the strings were of thin gut and their tension sufficiently low that the bridge could support their weight without caving in the belly or driving its feet through the wood. One of the commonest ways of seeking increased volume with all string instruments is to increase the string tension, and it is this increased tension that leads to greater weight on the bridge and the necessity both for the bass bar as reinforcement of the belly beneath it and for the sound post as a girder to hold the belly up. Incidental advantages are that the bass bar helps to diffuse the vibrations of the bridge along the belly and that the sound post transmits these vibrations to the back, but these functions, important as they are today in producing the tone to which we are accustomed on both viols and violins, are secondary to their original purpose, which was to prevent the collapse of the instrument.

The viols were usually played as a consort and the only one found at all frequently either as a solo instrument or playing with members of other families was the bass viol; this is why, in English, viola da gamba is usually taken to mean the bass viol unless the context makes it clear that the whole family is under discussion. As time went on, the full size bass was used only in the consort, while two smaller basses, the lyra viol and the division viol and their continental equivalents, were used for solo playing.

Plate 85 VIOLS (VIOLE DA GAMBA)
Left to right: tenor and bass viols
by Antonio Ciciliano, Venice,
c. 1550, C 75 & 77; tenor
viol by Francesco Linarol, Venice,
c. 1550, C 71; violone or great
bass viol by Ventura Linarol,
Padua, 1585, C 78.
(*Kunsthistorisches Museum,
Vienna*)

The Violins

The culmination of the mediaeval fiddle, which was still in use in Memling's time, about 1480 (plate IX, right hand side) was the lira da braccio. This usually had five strings on the fingerboard and two drone strings running beside the neck (plate 86), the drones usually being tuned in octaves and treated as one string. It has frequently been suggested that the lira da braccio was the ancestor of the violin, for the shape of the two instruments is very similar, but, as David Boyden has established, the violin, or, to be more exact, a proto-violin, existed at least as early as the lira da braccio. It is clear, though, that as the violin was developed, it drew on the lira da braccio

for many of its features and to that extent, the suggestions of influence are true. The violin seems to be the result of combining some features of the rebec with others of the lira da braccio and it owes its existence to the continuing need for a treble string instrument which could combine agility with volume. The technique of the viol has never been clumsy, but nevertheless, agility is not an expression that one would associate with the viol, nor is the viol a loud instrument. Equally, both viols and lira da braccio were large instruments, the smallest member of the viol family being as big as a viola, the alto violin. And so the violin came into being, originally as an instrument with three strings, like the rebecs, but with a larger body and hence more

Plate 86 Lira da braccio by
Giovanni Maria da Brescia,
Venice, *c.* 1525. (*Hill Collection 8,
Ashmolean Museum, Oxford*)

volume, primarily as an instrument for dance music
and other informal occasions. David Boyden has
identified plate XI, Gaudenzio Ferrari's 'Madonna
of the Orange Trees' of 1529 or 1530, as the first
illustration to show a violin. Another illustration, at
least ten and perhaps twenty years earlier is plate 62
in which the player to the right of the harpist is
playing a hybrid instrument which is closer to the
violin than to anything else. The upper bouts are
those of a violin, although the lower bouts have no
corners; there are four strings and a violin-type
bridge and tail piece, although the sound holes are
C-shaped, like those of a viol or fiddle.

It took surprisingly little time for the violin to
establish its classic form. Boyden quotes descriptions
from 1556 of violin, viola and violoncello, with the
same tunings for the four strings that we use. By
1564, Andrea Amati in Cremona was building
violins (plate 87) and by 1574, violas (plate 88) for
Charles IX of France, who ordered a complete set of
these instruments from Amati, twelve large violins,
twelve small, six violas and eight basses, which were
presumably violoncellos. Of these, one of the small
violins and one of the violas are preserved in Oxford,
and are illustrated here. At the end of the eighteenth
century, more sound and a greater range were
required of the violin family also, and instruments
were fitted with new, longer necks which were
canted back to increase the string tension, higher
bridges and longer finger boards. The violin in plate
87 has been converted in this way, whereas the viola
in plate 88 has been restored to its original state; the
internal modifications of heavier bass bar and sound
post are not, of course, visible in the plates.

The viola was built in two main sizes, of which
this is the larger, both of which were tuned to the
same pitches. The smaller was used for the higher
parts and the larger for the lower, the size of the body
being suited to the resonance required. The bridge of
this instrument is modern; a painting showing an
old bridge can be seen in plate XII.

The evidence is clear that the viole da braccio, or
violins, and the viole da gamba, or viols, were
contemporary with each other, practically from the
beginning, for there are less than twenty years
between their first appearances. The differences
between them are in their construction and thus in
their tone quality and hence in their use. The viol

Plate 87 (*Left*) Violin made for Charles IX of France by Andrea Amati, Cremona, 1564. Modern neck, finger board and tail piece. Length of body 342 mm. (*Hill Collection 10*)

Plate 88 Viola made for Charles IX by Andrea Amati in 1574. Neck, finger board and tail piece reconstructed in original style. Length of body 470 mm. (*Hill Collection 11*)

Plate 89 LUTES
Left to right: mean lute, 1582,
C 36; treble lute or quintern,
C 39; mandore, C 41. All by
Wendelin Tieffenbrucker,
Padua. (*Kunsthistorisches Museum,
Vienna*)

had no bass bar or sound post; its belly was arched in a smooth and gentle curve from side to side; its body was deeper than that of a violin of the same size; the belly and back fitted exactly to the ribs and did not overhang the sides; there were frets tied round the neck and across the finger board; there were six strings, as a rule, tuned in fourths and a third, similarly to those of the lute; the bow was held with the palm outwards so that the two strokes, up-bow and down-bow, were nearly equal in strength, the up-bow, the pushing stroke, being slightly the stronger. The violin, on the other hand, had a sound post and a bass bar from the beginning, so far as we can tell; both belly and back were much more strongly arched, as can be seen in plate XI, and the arching starts from part way across both plates, rather than from the edge; there were no frets; there were only four strings, which were tuned in fifths; the bow was held with the palm inwards so that the two strokes were very different in strength, the down-bow, the pulling stroke, being much the stronger. The presence of sound post and bass bar and the strong arching of the belly suggests also that the four strings of the violin exerted greater pressure on the bridge than the six strings of the viol and thus that the string tension, and hence the volume, was greater for that reason as well as because of the more forceful bowing technique and the greater resonance

Plate 90 BASS LUTES
Left to right: Paduan theorbo by
Wendelin Tieffenbrucker, 1595
(*Kunsthistorisches Museum,
Vienna, A46*); Venetian theorbo
by Matteo Sellas, 1637 (*Victoria
& Albert Museum, London,
1126–1869*); Roman theorbo,
archlute or chitarrone by Magno
Tieffenbrucker, Venice, second
half of 16th century.
(*Kunsthistorisches Museum,
Vienna, C45*)

of a box with a sound post. The extinction of the viols came well after our period, but all this evidence makes it amply clear that it was due to the changing style and taste of music, rather than to any superiority of the violin or inferiority of the viol. There were, and there are, things that the viol can do better than any other instrument; there were and there are things that the violin can do better than any other instrument. It so happened that late in the seventeenth century, tastes went the violin's way and not the viol's way and have continued further in that direction ever since.

The Lutes

The lute maintained and increased its importance as the queen of instruments. It has been said that Laux Maler fixed its classic form and comparison between his lute in plate XIII and Arnault de Zwolle's in plate 51 will show the changes between them, although the Maler has a wider neck than it had originally. The new lute is more pear-shaped, with the widest part of the body much lower down, only just above the bridge instead of near the mid-point. The lute, like all other instruments, was built in families; three instruments by Wendelin Tieffenbrucker are shown in plate 89: a mean, or normal, lute, a descant lute, the equivalent of the quintern of Maximilian (plate 62) and Virdung and an octave lute, the forerunner of the pandurina or Milanese mandolin which are, as Anthony Baines suggests, better called mandores. Larger lutes were also used, though these were a little later in their development. It would be tempting to speculate that the left-hand instrument in plate 90 was the earliest in type, the length needed for the bass strings being achieved by the enormous body added to a neck of normal proportions, the maker then realising that the same string length could be obtained more easily and more cheaply by fitting a long neck to a smaller body, as in the centre. Regrettably, we know too little about the origin of the theorbo for this to be anything but speculation. There are thought to have been two main streams, the one Paduan, Bolognese or Venetian, the two left-hand instruments, and the other Roman, the chitarrone to the right, though the principal makers of both were Germans or Austrians who had settled in Italy. The theorbo was a large-bodied lute with a crooked extension to the head which carried additional bass strings which ran beside the neck and were not stopped on the finger board. The chitarrone had a body of more normal size, often made from an older mean lute, but with a very long, straight extension to carry the open bass strings.

At much the same time, the end of the sixteenth century, ordinary lutes were also altered. The left-hand instrument on plate 89 is probably in original condition, with five double courses; the lute was usually strung so, with two strings to each pitch. The Laux Maler (plate XIII) was re-necked in the first half of the seventeenth century with a much wider finger board and a new head carrying eleven double courses and two single courses, the highest of which is tuned by a peg riding above the main peg box. The upper courses would be tuned to the normal pitches, the lower courses being tuned as basses in whole tone steps. Dowland's lute songs and lute pieces were written for such a disposition, which had the advantage over the theorbo and chitarrone that although the bass strings were thicker than was desirable for the best tone, the instrument was far less unwieldy.

The Cittern

It is traditional when referring to the lute to quote the old canard that an eighty-year-old lutenist had spent sixty years tuning his lute. Things were not quite so bad as that story implies, for a well maintained lute could be tuned quite quickly and should not need retuning any more frequently than a violin. However, no violinist ever sits down to play without tuning his instrument and no more could a lutenist embark on an evening's enjoyment without a thorough tune-up. This was partly because of the extreme lightness of the lute's construction, for a good lute feels almost like a feather in the hand and quivers in response to a spoken word, and partly because of the use of thin gut strings, especially in the treble, which were considerably affected by changes of temperature and humidity. For more casual music-making, for the customers in barbers' shops and taverns, instruments were required which could be reached down from the wall and played straight away. This need was filled by the cittern, an instrument with wire strings which held their tuning and a flat back which was far more robust than the

delicate pear-shaped body of the lute. A normal cittern would also cost less than a lute, for the body was made of two flat plates separated by tapering ribs, narrowing towards the bottom, instead of being built up from slender curved staves like the lute. More expensive citterns were also made, such as the one by Girolamo de Virchis, arguably the world's most beautiful musical instrument, made for Archduke Ferdinand of the Tyrol (plate XIV); such an instrument would cost more than any lute and ease of playing was also a consideration in the comparison of lute and cittern.

Both the body tapering towards the bottom and the small wings at the root of the neck have been recognised by Dr Winternitz as vestigial traces of the gittern. By the sixteenth century, the four strings of the gittern had been increased to six double courses, usually with a re-entrant tuning like that of the ukelele, and the tied gut frets of the gittern had been replaced with fixed brass frets, for the wire strings would speedily cut frets of gut.

Like the lute, the cittern was made in larger sizes, some resembling the bass lutes, such as the ceterone which resembled the chitarrone. Others were distinct instruments in their own right, such as the orpharion (plate 91), the bandora or pandora and the polyphant or stump. Many of these were made in elaborate, festooned shapes, like the Rose orpharion. Such instruments were used both for solo playing and for ensembles, but their life was fairly short, perhaps because the extra strings defeated the initial purpose of the instrument, to provide a substitute for the lute which would be easier to tune and play, and perhaps because of the introduction of the guitar which had a deeper body and a more resonant tone.

The treble cittern reappeared in the late eighteenth century as the English and Portuguese guitars and exists today under the name of the flat-backed mandolin; the Neapolitan mandolin is, to all intents and purposes, a cittern with a lute-like back.

Plate 92 Vihuela marked Gvadelvpe. Six double courses; the bridge is missing and the mark on the belly is not the original position. Spanish, probably early 16th century. (*Musée Jacquemart-André, Paris*)

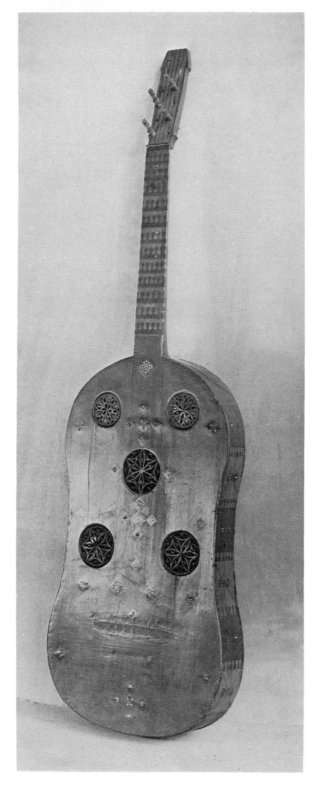

Vihuela and Guitar

The guitar was a Spanish instrument, developed from the vihuela, a unique specimen of which survives in Paris (plate 92). Michael Prynne, in his study of this instrument, hazards no guess as to its date, saying only that it corresponds with sixteenth-century illustrations. The vihuela was the basic instrument which led to the fiddle, viol and viola, as the guitar is still called in Portugal (guitarra is the cittern-like instrument referred to above). By the sixteenth century, the guitar was becoming popular throughout Europe, often called, as Daniel Heartz points out, the gittern, usually with four and occasionally with five courses, as against the six that were customary on the vihuela. The appearance of the early guitars will be familiar from paintings by Watteau and others; they were narrower than the vihuela, but much deeper in the body and with only one sound hole. They were popular with all levels of society, as the story of Mary Queen of Scots and Rizzio indicates. There were two main types, the normal finger played instrument which was gut strung and the chitarra battente, a wire strung instrument with a slightly rounded back, which was played with a plectrum.

The Harp

The harp is the only instrument which was used throughout the period covered by this book. Like the lute, it was used both as a solo instrument and in ensembles and by the late sixteenth century, when only the largest bass lutes were able to sustain an ensemble, the harp was able to grow and to continue to be of use. Since some of the strings in Maximilian's harp (plate 62) are hidden one cannot be sure of the range of that instrument, but plate 93 (left) makes it clear that by the third quarter of the century the range was over three octaves, although the compass was still diatonic. The brays in the belly can be seen clearly in this photograph. At much this time, the harp made its first great leap into the future. A second row of strings was added which could be tuned to the 'black' notes, so rendering the instrument chromatic. Plate 93 (right) shows a harp of this type, with a stepped neck so that the strings from the upper row of tuning pins start to the left of those in the lower row, then pass between them and

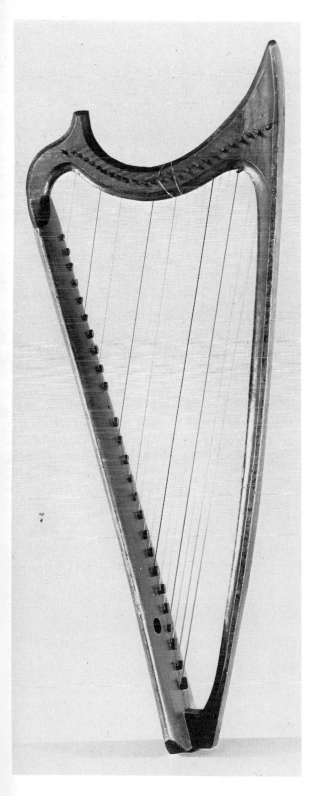

Plate 93 *Right:* Arpa doppia, chromatic harp with two ranks of strings. Italian, 17th century. (*Kunsthistorisches Museum, Vienna*) *Left:* Diatonic harp with single rank of strings and L-shaped brays. German, early 16th century. (*Germanisches Nationalmuseum, Nürnberg, MI 59*)

Plate 94　Clavichord by Onesto Tosi, Genoa, 1568. Fretted with 22 double courses for 45 keys. Three sound board bridges. (*Museum of Fine Arts, Boston, 17.1796*)

are pegged to the right-hand side of the belly. The strings thus form a narrow X and all are accessible to either hand. It was an instrument of this type that Monteverdi demanded as the Arpa Doppia in his opera, *Orfeo*. A third rank was added shortly afterwards, making the triple harp which was the standard instrument through the seventeenth and eighteenth centuries and which survived as a folk instrument in Wales.

The harp was thus able to provide full chords as an accompanying and continuo instrument. We tend, today, to think of the organ and the harpsichord as the only continuo instruments, those used to play a bass line with suitable chords above it to fill out the harmonies of the music. In the period when the continuo was a living tradition and the foundation of all music, from the sixteenth to the early nineteenth centuries, the large lutes, theorbo and chitarrone, the large citterns, bandora and ceterone, and the harp were also all regarded as acceptable continuo instruments, either by themselves or alternating, as in *Orfeo*, for contrast between one section and another.

Keyboard Instruments

The Clavichord

The clavichord no longer had a single choir of strings, all tuned to the same basic pitch. The instrument by Tosi of Genoa (plate 94) has three sound board bridges, instead of the one in Arnault's drawing (plate 43) and two hitch-pin bridges, those at the left-hand end, so that there were at least five basic pitches for the strings, which could be at more efficient tensions for the range of notes required from them. Each pair of strings is still shared by several tangents but there was far greater freedom of chordal movement than in the fifteenth century. It was not until the early eighteenth century that clavichords with a separate pair of strings for each note became general, and the fretted or gebunden clavichord, in which neighbouring tangents share a string, is being revived today as players come to appreciate the advantages of its lightness and of its ease of tuning and realise that very little of the true clavichord literature requires the ability to play simultaneously notes a semitone apart. Edwin Ripin

Plate 95   Single manual
harpsichord. Italian, mid–16th
century. (*Germanisches
Nationalmuseum, Nürnberg, MIR
1071*)

has observed that the sixteenth-century clavichord was more efficiently designed in other respects also, with a more effective sound board and better bridges, which produced a more even tone over the compass of the instrument.

The Harpsichord and Virginals

The harpsichord also changed between Arnault's plan (plate 48) and the mid-sixteenth century (plate 95). There were two great centres of manufacture and development, one in the Low Countries, principally at Antwerp, and the other in Italy. Of the two, it seems to have been the Italians who led in the development of the harpsichord, whereas in Antwerp, so far as we can tell from surviving instruments, the initial emphasis was on the smaller instruments such as the virginals. It should, perhaps, be emphasised once again that the nomenclature of the keyboard instruments in this period, and later, is chaotic. The terms harpsichord, spinet and virginals, and their equivalents in other languages, were freely interchangeable. Today, for reference and descriptive purposes, it is agreed that harpsichord is reserved for the wing-shaped instrument, like our grand piano (plates 48 and 95). It was proposed by Alec Hodsdon and Cecil Clutton that virginals should be applied to that instrument with both bridges on the sound board and strings running parallel to the front board of the case, with jacks running diagonally across the sound board from the left front to the right rear (plates 96, 97 and 98). The name of spinet should be applied to those other small instruments which have one bridge on the wrest plank and one on the sound board and which therefore have their jacks running parallel to the front board and the strings running diagonally from front left to right rear; spinets are not illustrated here because this type of instrument was not introduced until the mid-seventeenth century. These two terms, virginals and spinet, would thus define two quite distinct types of small harpsichord, one, the virginals, being an instrument with its own characteristic tone colour, the other, the spinet, filling in its day the same rôle as the upright piano does for us, and they should be

applied for descriptive and reference purposes without any regard for the chaotic local terminology of earlier centuries; such modern usage would then distinguish clearly between two instruments whose construction, tone quality, acoustical behaviour and date were quite different.

A harpsichord is a sufficiently expensive piece of musical furniture that many were rebuilt and adapted as musical tastes changed. Thus, it is rare to find one in original condition, which has not had extra strings, extra rows of jacks, extra keyboards added to it. In addition, harpsichords became collectors' pieces at quite an early date, so that a minor industry sprang up, particularly in Italy, to supply the market, either by cobbling together bits of unrelated instruments to make one complete instrument, or by making old instruments from new. As a result of these two trends, many harpsichords of early date are not all that they seem to be. One of the earliest still in original state is a mid-sixteenth-century instrument in Nürnberg (plate 95), which was made in Italy with a single rank of strings. The range

appears to be from E to c''', but is in fact from C to c'''. This was achieved by the use of the short octave: of the lowest keys, the normal E key sounds C, the F sharp key sounds D, the G sharp key sounds E and the others produce the notes to which we are accustomed. There was seldom any demand for the lowest C, D, F and G sharps and this arrangement was therefore both practical and practicable. Some more elaborate instruments were built with split black notes, so that the front half of the key sounded the normal short octave pitch and the back part sounded the chromatic note that would be expected from that key in other parts of the range.

At the end of the sixteenth century, the Flemish harpsichords were becoming established in a style very different from the Italian. The Italian instruments were lightly built, almost entirely of cypress wood, with a light, undecorated inner case which was inserted into the painted or leather-covered outer case for storage or transport, whereas the Flemish instruments were more heavily built with a single case. The tone quality of the instruments was quite different, partly for this reason and partly because the scaling, the length of the strings for each pitch, and thus the string weight and tension, was different, as was the construction of the sound board. The Flemish instruments were often built with two keyboards, double manual harpsichords, as on the left-hand side of plate XV. The two manuals did not provide a choice of tone colours, plucking on different ranks of strings as on the later seventeenth and eighteenth-century harpsichords, but were designed to aid in transposition, usually by a fourth. The keys of the lower manual are usually set so that the F keys pluck the same strings as the C keys on the upper manual and so on, throughout the compass of the instrument. So many of these instruments were made, and a member of the famous Ruckers family so adamantly refused to make a double manual harpsichord with any other disposition for Charles I of England (Raymond Russell quotes the relevant correspondence), that there must have been a constant demand for this transposing facility. We can only presume that there were two recognised pitches, akin to the Chorton and Kammerton of the succeeding century, and that this arrangement permitted players to play in either without the trouble of transposing.

Italian and Flemish virginals also differed. The Italian instruments were usually polygonal in shape with the keyboard projecting from the long side. The earliest known Flemish instrument (plate 96) has many Italian features, and is polygonal in shape, though with a recessed keyboard, but, as Ripin pointed out in his article on the instrument, details of the mechanism are more Flemish than Italian. The true Flemish style was quite different, as can be seen from two very typical instruments (plates 97 and 98). The instrument was rectangular, instead of polygonal; the casework was heavier; more important, a true second manual was provided. The small virginals, which can be seen projecting from its storage drawer to one side of the main keyboard on both plates, could be taken out and laid on top of the case so that the jacks of the main keyboard could pass through slots in the bottom of the small instrument and activate the jacks of that instrument also. It sounded an octave higher than the main instrument and thus added brightness to the virginals' somewhat hollow tone and could also be played independently from its own keyboard. There were two types of Flemish virginals, the normal instrument (plate 97) whose jacks plucked fairly close to the left-hand bridge and whose keyboard is therefore towards the left-hand side, and the muselaar (plate 98) whose jacks plucked almost in the centre of the string, thus tending to eliminate the even-numbered harmonics (see p. 76) from the sound spectrum, producing a much hollower, almost clarinet-like tone, and whose keyboard is therefore in the centre.

The Regals

The regals is a small reed organ whose reeds are not dependent upon pipes for their pitch, as are, for example, the trumpet and other reed stops of the normal organ, but which have small resonators attached to them, the various shapes of which affect the tone; the reed itself, which is a beating reed and which must not be confused with the free reed of the nineteenth-century harmonium, is responsible for its own pitch. Many of the shapes of resonator were small in size, so that the regals could be built into a pipe organ, taking little space, or could exist on its own, either as an instrument in the shape of a very small positive (eg behind Hofhaimer's back in plate 61) or in so small a compass that the whole thing, reeds, bellows, keyboard and all, could be folded up into a case designed to look like a large bible. The bible regal was in use in the sixteenth century, although almost all extant examples are later in date. The regals had a biting, snarling sound which could be used either to give an edge to the rather gentle sound of the positive or to depict a dramatic character in opera, as Monteverdi uses it for Charon, the boatman of the dead, in *Orfeo*. Its pungent tone also enabled a small regals to support singers more strongly than a small pipe organ, so that it became a useful instrument for small chapels and households, taking up little space and costing less than a pipe organ; it was thus the sixteenth- and seventeenth-century equivalent of the nineteenth-century harmonium and the twentieth-century electronic organ.

The Organ

The smallest organ, the portative, seems to have died out by this time, and among the last illustrations to show it are plate X and Raphael's famous St Cecilia,

another example of the reversed keyboard with the bass pipes to the player's right, as Jack Schuman has pointed out. The positive was still popular (plate 61) and the large church organ grew very considerably in the sixteenth century. Plate 99 shows an organ now in Middelberg but originally built for the Nicolaikerk in Utrecht. The main body of the organ was built about 1480 and then looked very much like those in plates 50 and 58, both of which are some fifty years earlier. The upper work was modified in 1547 and the back-positive, the whole section behind the player's back, was added in 1590. Finally, a pedal was added in about 1600, bringing the organ into the state in which it is seen today. It will be observed that some of the pipes are inverted, a not-uncommon device in Dutch organs of this period, which seems

to have been purely aesthetic in intention although, as Guy Oldham has observed, it does help to keep the dust and the dead birds out of the pipes.

The Orchestra

All these keyboard instruments were used by themselves for solo music. The organs were used also to accompany the voices in the choir and both organs and harpsichords were used to play the bass lines and to fill out the harmonies in the new combination of instruments which was just coming into being, the orchestra. The great musical combination of the Renaissance was, as we have already observed, the consort. Before this conception of homogeneous tone colour, the group of different sizes of like instruments, had come into being, ensemble music

Plate 99   Organ by Peter
Gerritz, 1479–80; upperwork
added by Cornelius Gerritz,
1547; back positive added 1590;
pedals added c. 1600. (*Originally
in the Nicolaikerk, Utrecht; now in
the Koorkerk, Middelberg*)

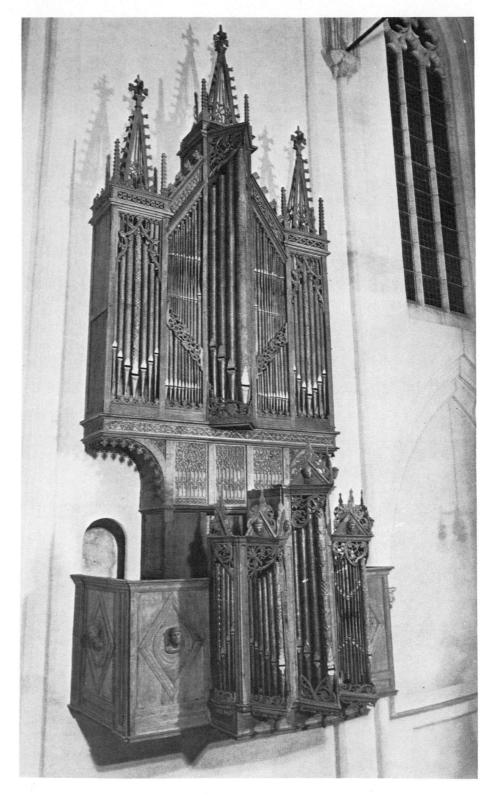

had been played by miscellaneous groups of instruments, whatever had been available or convenient, as can be seen from many illustrations in this book, from that on the dust jacket onwards. With the Renaissance, all these casual conglomerations of instrumental sonorities gave way to order and to evenness of tone colour. The fascinating thing about this is for how short a time it lasted. While Dowland was writing his *Lachrimae* for five viols, Morley was publishing his *Consort Lessons* for broken consort, the usual English term for a mixed bag of instruments, and even before that date mixed bands such as those in plates 60 and 62 were quite common. The final stroke that finished the whole consort was the rise of the opera.

The masque, the drama with musical interludes which were sung or danced and which was popular in the sixteenth century, gave way to an entertainment which was musical throughout. Since there were now no lengthy passages of spoken dialogue interspersed among the musical interludes, more musical variety was required and this implied more instruments in order to vary the sonority of the music. One of the first operas with specified instrumental forces, as distinct from music in parts for unspecified instruments, is Monteverdi's *Orfeo*, produced first in Mantua in 1607. This requires a large force of instrumentalists, consisting of two harpsichords, two contrabass violins (double basses), ten violins (ten members of the violin family, probably four violins, four violas and two cellos), a double harp, two French-style small violins (possibly what we call violini piccoli but probably, since they accompany the shepherds, the older rebecs), three chitarroni, one ceterone, two positive organs, one regals, three bass viols and a contrabass viol, five trombones, two cornetts, a sopranino recorder and two other small recorders, four trumpets (though there are five parts) and probably timpani as suggested above. Many of the orchestral ritornelli through the work have their instrumental composition specified, as have a number of the accompaniments to the singers and, above the first piece of music, the 'Toccata', the composer directs that it is to be played three times before the curtain rises with all the instruments; the only word that we have available to translate *tutti li stromenti* is orchestra.

The word, used in our sense of a combination of instruments, was unknown, as, for most of another century, was the idea of a single group of players producing contrasting tone colours at the dictate of a composer, but all the material was available, as may be seen in plate XV. Here, in Breughel's 'Allegory of the Sense of Hearing', painted just after the end of our period, we have all the constituents of the whole consorts, of the broken consorts, of domestic music making, of casual noise making, of the hunting field and of the orchestra. At the extreme left we see the pipes of an organ and a double manual harpsichord, probably by one of the Ruckers family of Antwerp; at the extreme right we see whistles and hunting horns. Between them are all the instruments of the day, omitting only the crumhorn and the cittern of all that we have surveyed in this last century. In our imaginations, we can group these instruments as we wish; we can look back to the days of the consort, or we can look forward into the seventeenth and eighteenth centuries, when our orchestras, our modern music, began.

Acknowledgements

Over the years, more people than I can count, most of them members
of the Galpin Society, the main international organisation for the study
of musical instruments, have provided knowledge, references and
information, all of which has contributed to this book. Of them, I
would like to thank, in particular, Guy Oldham, who has always been
ready to give clear answers to any problem, and Michael Morrow, who
not only introduced me to medieval music and encouraged me to play
it properly and to reconstruct instruments on which to do so, but who
also referred me to Henry Holland Carter's *Dictionary* and to the
manuscript Sloane 3983 (plates II and III) in the British Library. I am
grateful to all the photographers who have allowed me to use their
pictures, and in particular to Axel Poignant who suffered gross discomfort
and inconvenience to help me. Michael Evans of the Warburg Institute
was a tower of strength and introduced me to many iconographic sources
and I am more than grateful to him. Finally, I must thank both my
elder daughter, who has corrected my English, and my wife who has
not only corrected my history but who can decipher medieval hand-
writing and translate the result into English; many improvements to
this book are to their credit; such blemishes as remain are to my blame.

Bibliography

Abbreviations: GSJ—*The Galpin Society Journal;* EM— *Early Music*

Adam de la Halle. *Oeuvres Complètes,* ed E. de Coussemaker (Paris, 1872; reprinted Gregg, Farnborough, 1966)

Adkins, C. J. 'Investigation of the sound-producing mechanism of the jew's harp', *Journal of the Acoustical Society of America,* 55 no 3 (March, 1974), 667–670

Agricola, Martin. *Musica instrumentalis deudsch* (Wittemberg, 1528; reprinted Breitkopf & Härtel, Leipzig, 1896)

Andersson, Otto. *The Bowed-Harp* (Reeves, 1930)

Arbeau, Thoinot. *Orchésographie* (Langres, 1589; reprinted in Mary Stewart Evans's translation, Dover, New York, 1966)

Arnault de Zwolle, Henri. Bibliothèque Nationale, Paris, MS latin 7295. Published in Latin and French translation in G. le Cerf and E. R. Labande, *Instruments de musique au xve siècle: les traités d'Henri-Arnaut de Zwolle et de diverses anonymes* (Paris, 1932; reprinted Bärenreiter, Kassel)

Bachmann, Werner. *The Origins of Bowing* (O.U.P. 1969)

Baines, Anthony. *Bagpipes* (Pitt Rivers Museum, Oxford, 1960)

——. *European and American Musical Instruments* (Batsford, 1966)

——. *Non-Keyboard Instruments* (Victoria & Albert Museum, Catalogue of Musical Instruments, vol. 2, H.M.S.O., 1968)

——. *Woodwind Instruments and their History* (3rd ed, Faber & Faber, 1967)

——. (ed) *Musical Instruments Through the Ages* (2nd ed, Penguin and Faber & Faber, 1966)

Bessaraboff, Nicholas. *Ancient European Musical Instruments* (Museum of Fine Arts, Boston, 1941)

Besseler, Heinrich. *Musik des Mittelalters und der Renaissance* (Handbuch der Musikwissenschaft, Potsdam, 1931)

Blades, James. *Percussion Instruments and their History* (2nd ed, Faber & Faber, 1975)

——. *Early Percussion Instruments from the Middle Ages to the Baroque* (O.U.P., 1976)

——. and Jeremy Montagu. 'Capriol's Revenge', *EM* 1 no 2 (1973), 84–92

Boyden, David. *Catalogue of The Hill Collection of Musical Instruments in the Ashmolean Museum, Oxford* (O.U.P., 1969)

——. *The History of Violin Playing from its origins to 1761,* (O.U.P., 1965)

Bridge, Joseph. 'Horns', *Journal of the Chester & North Wales Architectural, Archaeological and Historical Society,* ns 11 (1905), 85–166

Buchner, Alexandr. *Mechanical Musical Instruments* (Batchworth, nd)

——. *Musical Instruments: an Illustrated History* (2nd ed of *Musical Instruments Through the Ages* (Octopus, 1973)

——. *Zaniklé Dřevéné Dechové Nástroje 16 století;* 'The extinct wooden instruments of the 16th century, Acta Musei Nationalis Pragae, Vol. VII A–Hist. 2, Prague, 1952)

Bunt, Cyril G. E. *The Horn of Ulf* (York Minster, nd)

Carter, Henry Holland. *A Dictionary of Middle English Musical Terms* (Indiana U.P., 1961; reprinted Kraus, New York, 1968)

Clutton, Cecil. 'Arnault's MS', *GSJ* 5 (1952), 3–8

Crane, Frederick. *Extant Medieval Musical Instruments* (Iowa U.P., 1972)

Dart, Thurston. 'Review of Thomas Morley, *The First Book of Consort Lessons,* ed Sydney Beck', *GSJ* 13 (1960), 98–102

Davison, M. H. Armstrong. 'A Note on the History of the Northumbrian Small Pipes', *GSJ* 22 (1969), 78–80

de Hen, Ferd. J. 'Folk Instruments of Belgium: Part I', *GSJ* 25 (1972), 87–132

Dowland, John. *Lachrimae* (1605; transcribed Peter Warlock, O.U.P., 1927)

Early Music, 1973– . Published quarterly by O.U.P.

Farmer, Henry George. *Islam* (Musikgeschichte in Bildern, Bd 3, lief 2, Deutscher Verlag für Musik, Leipzig, nd)

——. *The Organ of the Ancients, from Eastern Sources* (1931)

Galpin, Francis W. *Old English Instruments of Music* (4th ed, revised Thurston Dart, Methuen, 1965)

The Galpin Society Journal, 1948– . Published annually, for the study of musical instruments, from Chesham Bois, Amersham, Buckinghamshire

Hardy, Charles Frederic. 'On the Music in the Painted Glass of the Windows in the Beauchamp Chapel at Warwick', *Archaeologia* 61 pt 2 (1909), 583–600

Harwood, Ian. 'A Fifteenth-Century Lute Design', *Lute Society Journal* 2 (1960)

——. 'An introduction to renaissance viols', *EM* 2 no 4 (1974), 235–246

Hayes, Gerald R. *The Viols and other bowed instruments* (O.U.P., 1930; reprinted Broude, New York, 1969)

Heartz, Daniel. 'An Elizabethan Tutor for the Guitar', *GSJ* 16 (1963), 3–21

Henry VIII. 'Inventory of the Guarderobes, etc' (1547), British Library, Harley 1419 (list of musical instruments printed in Galpin. *Old English Instruments* and Russell, *Harpsichord & Clavichord*)

Hodsdon, Alec and Cecil Clutton. 'Defining the Virginal', *The Musical Times*, 1251 (May 1947), 153–154

Hughes-Hughes, Augustus. *Catalogue of the Manuscript Music in the British Museum*, vol 3 with list of drawings of instruments in manuscripts (British Museum, 1909)

Kinsky, Georg. *Geschichte der Musik in Bildern* (Leipzig, 1929; also in English, French and Italian)

Ling, Jan. *Nyckelharpan* (Musikhistoriska Museet, Stockholm, 1967)

Mahillon, Victor-Charles. *Catalogue descriptif et analytique du Musée Instrumental du Conservatoire Royal de Musique de Bruxelles* (Ghent and Brussels, for the museum, 1880–1922)

Maximilian I. *The Triumph* (1526; reprinted Dover, New York, 1964)

Merlin, François and Jacques Cellier. 'Recherche de Plusieurs Singularités', Bibliothèque Nationale, Paris, ms français 9152

Mersenne, Marin. *Harmonie Universelle* (Paris, 1636; reprinted Centre Nationale de Recherche Scientifique, Paris, 1963)

Montagu, Jeremy *Making Early Percussion Instruments* (O.U.P. 1976)

——. 'Early Percussion Techniques', *EM* 2 no 1 (1974), 20–24

——. 'On the Reconstruction of Mediaeval Instruments of Percussion', *GSJ* 23 (1970), 104–114

Monteverdi, Claudio. *L'Orfeo* (Venice, 1609; ed G. F. Malipiero, Chester, London, 1923)

Morley, Thomas. *The First Book of Consort Lessons* (1599; ed Sydney Beck, Peters, New York, 1959)

New Oxford History of Music. 2, 'Early Medieval Music up to 1300'

——. 3, 'Ars Nova and the Renaissance' (O.U.P., 1954 and 1960)

Panum, Hortense. *The Stringed Instruments of the Middle Ages* (Reeves, nd)

Pegge, R. Morley. *The French Horn* (Benn, 1960)

——. 'The "Anaconda" ', *GSJ* 12 (1959), 53–56

Perrot, Jean. *The Organ from its Invention in the Hellenistic Period to the end of the Thirteenth Century* (O.U.P., 1971)

Praetorius, Michael. *Syntagmatis Musici 2: de Organographia* (Wolfenbüttel, 1619; reprinted Bärenreiter, Kassel, 1958)

Prynne, Michael. 'A Surviving Vihuela de Mano', *GSJ* 16 (1963), 22–27

Reese, Gustave. *Music in the Middle Ages* (Norton, New York, 1940)

——. *Music in the Renaissance* (Norton, New York, 2nd ed, 1959)

Rimmer, Joan. *The Irish Harp* (Irish Cultural Relations Committee, Cork, 1969)

——. 'The Morphology of the Irish Harp', *GSJ* 17 (1964), 39–49

——. 'The Morphology of the Triple Harp', *GSJ* 18 (1965), 90–103

Ripin, Edwin M. 'The Early Clavichord', *Musical Quarterly* 53 no 4 (October, 1967), 518–538

——. 'On Joes Karest's Virginal and the Origins of the Flemish Tradition', *Keyboard Instruments; Studies in Keyboard Organology*, ed E. M. Ripin (Edinburgh U.P., 1971), 65–73

Russell, Raymond. *The Harpsichord and Clavichord* (Faber & Faber, 1959)

——. *Keyboard Instruments* (Victoria & Albert Museum, Catalogue of Musical Instruments, vol 1, H.M.S.O., 1968)

Sachs, Curt. *Handbuch der Musikinstrumentenkunde* (Breitkopf & Härtel, Leipzig, 1930)

——. *The History of Musical Instruments* (Norton, New York, 1940)

——. *Sammlung alter Musikinstrumente bei der staatlichen Hochschule für Musik zu Berlin* (Berlin, 1922)

Sárosi, Bálint. *Die Volksmusikinstrumente Ungarns*, Handbuch der europäischen Volksmusikinstrumente, Series I, Bd 1 (DVf M, Leipzig, nd)

Sauerlandt, Max. *Die Musik in fünf Jahrhunderten der Europäischen Malerei* (Langewiesche, Leipzig, 1922)

Schlosser, Julius. *Die Sammlung alter Musikinstrumente, Kunsthistorisches Museum in Wien* (Vienna, 1920)

Schuman, Jack C. ' "Reversed" Portatives and Positives in Early Art', *GSJ* 24 (1971), 16–21

Seebass, Tilman. *Musikdarstellung und Psalterillustration im früheren Mittelalter* (Francke, Bern, 1973)

Tinctoris, Johannes. *De Inventione et Usu Musicae*. Excerpts on instruments translated by Anthony Baines in *GSJ* 3 (1950), 19–26

Virdung, Sebastian. *Musica Getutscht* (Basel, 1511; reprinted Bärenreiter, Kassel, 1970)

Winternitz, Emanuel. 'The Survival of the Kithara and the Evolution of the English Cittern', *Journal of the Warburg and Courtauld Institutes* 24 no 3–4 (1961) (reprinted in Winternitz, *Musical Instruments and their Symbolism in Western Art*, Faber & Faber, 1967)

Index